Open your heart to love
and inspire others through
life's challenges!

"Don't Stop Be-Lee-V!"

Will Lee

My WALK with Hue

A Story of Tragedy, Love, and Triumph

WILLIAM M. LEE

WESTBOW
PRESS®
A DIVISION OF THOMAS NELSON
& ZONDERVAN

Scriptures taken from the Holy Bible, New International Version®, NIV®. Copyright © 1973, 1978, 1984, 2011 by Biblica, Inc.™ Used by permission of Zondervan. All rights reserved worldwide. www.zondervan.com The "NIV" and "New International Version" are trademarks registered in the United States Patent and Trademark Office by Biblica, Inc.™

WestBow Press books may be ordered through booksellers or by contacting:

WestBow Press
A Division of Thomas Nelson & Zondervan
1663 Liberty Drive
Bloomington, IN 47403
www.westbowpress.com
1 (866) 928-1240

Because of the dynamic nature of the Internet, any web addresses or links contained in this book may have changed since publication and may no longer be valid. The views expressed in this work are solely those of the author and do not necessarily reflect the views of the publisher, and the publisher hereby disclaims any responsibility for them.

Any people depicted in stock imagery provided by Thinkstock are models, and such images are being used for illustrative purposes only. Certain stock imagery © Thinkstock.

ISBN: 978-1-5127-7978-3 (sc)
ISBN: 978-1-5127-7979-0 (hc)
ISBN: 978-1-5127-7977-6 (e)

Library of Congress Control Number: 2017904044

Print information available on the last page.

WestBow Press rev. date: 03/21/2017

To my wife, Tracy.

You have been the light in my life. We grew up together while raising a baby. You always see the best in people, even when they don't show it. You are my foundation in life, and you create purity for me on which to base all other relationships. You have been tested by family that can't see what you see, yet there you stand, solid in your faith and love. I would not be who I am today if you weren't in my life. Our life together, against all social norms and criticism, was meant to be as blessed as it has become. Thank you for being you.

I love you, Billy.

INTRODUCTION

*D*riving a car may be the ultimate metaphor for life. Some people stroll through the countryside at a leisurely pace while others drive hectically, weaving in and out of traffic, always in a hurry. Both may be okay, or both may be out of control. Even though they appear to be polar opposites, both can be missing exactly the same thing.

How many times do we focus on getting to a destination only to realize we've missed the journey? How many times do we drive and miss the signs along the way—signs telling us to slow down, speed up, be cautious, or stop altogether. When we' travel, do we need to make the decision to push forward through what looks like a treacherous situation, or do we need to make a U-turn. How many times are we so focused on the destination we get lost and find something new and exciting on a different route? No matter what happens, there are keys to our maps, even if the disciplines aren't in place to navigate our way through. At what point do we develop the disciplines, or do we use them only when it's convenient to us?

Life gives us signs. Have you ever looked at why some people go through tragedy and come through it stronger, but others wilt? Why do some people come from the depths of poverty to outperform those that have had every opportunity given to them? Why do people that fail in the same way, time after time, continue to weigh themselves down with guilt or blame others, including God, for their problems? Are the simple daily disciplines missing or undeveloped, or is it simpler than that? What I've come to know is that there is no magic bullet; there is only a will to succeed.

Through a life-altering event, my awakening happened. Four pillars of life were revealed, only for them to come crumbling down again to reveal the foundation for all life. This foundation has led me to personal triumph.

I think people overuse the word *miracle*. When you're going through a miracle, it typically goes unnoticed at the time, because it is all-encompassing. In those moments, a person can see only bits and pieces of the miracle that's continuing to evolve. An awakening allowed me to see miracles right before my eyes, even though the grand scale didn't become clear until years later. People were brought into my life at different times, which led to incredible growth and awareness. These miracles would have been missed—just like the signs we drive by every day—if I hadn't noticed the disciplines through ego-free growth, leaving me with an incredible view of God's perspective.

A clear chain of events runs through this story that I would have never recognized if my life had continued down the path I was on. I was comfortable with my life, and even through times of testing, I tried to return to that pathway.

This fictional story is based on real life events about a tragedy that changed my perspective. Not many people see the life around them every single moment of every day. The lessons we could see every day we typically ignore. We buzz by signs in our hurried, unaware lives and in retrospect don't recall being there in the first place. If you take the time to develop simple disciplines and search your own life, you'll see your unexamined journey. You will need daily reminders to fight for these disciplines and to keep God's incredible energy in front of you.

Three days before the tragedy, on July 3, 1998, Tracy and I celebrated our twelfth anniversary. Back then, it didn't stand out from any other day, but today it stands out as the last routine anniversary we would spend together.

If God truly puts signs in our lives to help us or guide us, then July 6, 1998, was a last-ditch effort to get me to stop and pay attention. A cliff lay ahead, but I didn't know it. Decisions would need to be made—or would they be overlooked and ignored? We face choices and decisions every day, but it was a tragedy that brought everything into perspective in a roaring millisecond.

———

As I was finishing this book, I received word that an old colleague had taken his own life. He had graduated from high school the same year I did, though he went to a competing school. We had similar jobs and in some aspects, parallel lives. I wish I had the opportunity to show him that life's grandeur is always there, even when your ego is telling you differently. How does life get clouded to the point that an ego decides to make its exit through an inability to show vulnerability? My heart goes out to his family. This tragedy left a beloved wife and three beautiful children behind. This book is also dedicated to them.

1

The Darkest of Shadows

A small Midwest town in central Michigan, Jackson was a mix of farms and businesses largely tied to the automotive industry in Detroit. If you traveled downtown, you were met by the sweet aroma of mineral spirits and industrial processes. Surrounding the city was plush farmland, often filled with corn or soybeans. It too offered its own set of smells, depending on the season—and some not so sweet.

My wife, Tracy, and I grew up in the small community of Spring Arbor, just west of Jackson. Tracy and I had a small home in an old neighborhood that backed up to Sandstone Creek. Her grandfather had helped build the house back in the 1960s, and her mother owned it until we bought it.

This small ranch had a unique feature that other houses in the neighborhood didn't have: a plush green path that Tracy's stepfather had made several years before. The path was like an oasis of green that cut through the marsh and ended at the creek. If you stood at the back of the house and looked down the hill, the view was always surreal, because no matter how dry or wet the season was, the path was always brilliantly green, surrounded by marsh flowers and cattails. It was like looking into nature's peacefulness, which could brighten any day. The path was about eight feet wide, and a row of massive willow trees lined the south side, standing like guardians of the pathway.

The path led to the edge of the creek, where an old wooden section of dock lay in the depths of mushy silt, cattail reeds, and flowering water lilies. This dilapidated piece of dock provided an extra six feet or so of walkway into the creek, where you could get an occasional glance at a perch or crawfish. There wasn't much creek left; marsh had grown in over the decades as the silt had settled, giving life to all the marsh flowers and sweet-smelling honeysuckle bushes.

An ordinary Monday in July, it was hot, and the air was dripping with moisture. As I came home from a long day at work, Tracy and I greeted each other in the kitchen with a quick kiss. "How was your day today?" she asked, then turned back to continue prepping for dinner.

As usual, I was ready to jump right into my routine, and as I headed downstairs to our bedroom on the lower level, I said, "Good, nothing special. I'm going to make it a short day at the gym so I can get started on the tree house tonight."

Not waiting for a response, I changed into my workout gear and ran back upstairs, grabbed my weightlifting gloves, gave Tracy a quick peck again, and shot off to the local college.

I had to sneak into the gym. By *sneaking* I mean I would walk in like I belonged there, greet the students working at the sign-in desk, and begin to warm up. Being six feet, 240 pounds, I wasn't much of a fly under the radar kind of guy. I had been going there so long that I had seen several generations of students and coaches come and go, so nobody knew if I belonged there or if I was in some sort of ten-year program.

My standard Monday workout didn't take much thought about what was next or how much weight to push. Fellow gym rats would usually step back to watch my bench routine. Whether it was smart or not, I had developed a system to work efficiently and alone that gave me the confidence to push a great amount of weight several times over. The people unacquainted with my routine would break into a sweat. All my routines were precise, efficient, and done with an unwavering calm. Perhaps it was preparing me for what was about to come. This workout was no different: warm up, push the weight, cool down, and drive back to the house.

That Monday would prove to be different from all others. I had purchased a chainsaw a week earlier to clean up some willow trees growing out back of our house. One in particular, in the center of the backyard, guarded the pathway entrance. It had become the target for a tree house for our kids.

The willow stared me down as I stood at the top of the hill, which sloped to the base of the beast. It stood as if it were a defiant soldier not willing to give ground. It clearly was the oldest of the trees, and it had battle wounds from years of weathering. With broken branches and battered limbs, the mighty willow's five-foot base secured it firmly to the ground. Six feet above its foundation, it broke into three separate trunks, each eighteen inches in diameter. It was a sturdy and massive foundation.

The plan in my head had me cutting those three trunks down, leaving about a foot of each one, and using the massive base for the floor support of the tree house.

Tracy and I have three kids, Ashley, Jacob, and Mackenzie. That evening, they were all with the neighbor, whose daughter baby-sat them when we went out on date nights. Tracy was cleaning up after dinner and getting ready for their return home from getting ice cream. They would need to get cleaned up and ready for bed.

Before showering from my workout, I decided to prep the giant willow so the upcoming weekend I could start building the tree house. With the evening approaching, the muggy air draped over the back yard, pulling the moisture from my body as if I stood in a sauna. I was so covered in sweat from the intense heat that I paid no attention to the bugs that thrive in it.

The first two trunks gave up easily and fell to the ground, clearing the way for that good solid base for the tree house. However, the third would give me a fight to remember. That third upper trunk was the most complete section of tree and required a more tactical approach.

There was a branch about ten feet off the ground, sticking straight out at a ninety-degree angle from the trunk. By "branch," I mean nine solid inches in diameter, extending nine feet out before spreading into several smaller branches. Tired and drenched, I traipsed up the hill to the garage and grabbed an old aluminum ladder. As I dragged the ladder out of the garage, Tracy yelled out of the screen door, "Be careful out there!"   Deep in thought, I was planning my next move. I knew what I needed to do. "Yep, I will!"

After laying the ladder up against the vertical trunk of the willow, I strapped it to the tree for a little extra safety and began the climb ten feet up. As I carried the saw up the ladder, I shifted my weight back and forth to make sure the ladder was secured to the tree. Leaning my body against the trunk, I reached across to the branch and got a good secure footing. Then I gave the saw one solid pull. The thick air, now polluted with the distinct sound of the chainsaw and smell of oil-bleached gas, was soon filled with thousands of tiny wood chips being extracted by the teeth of the saw.

In the meantime, Tracy had gone out front to meet the kids and thank the neighbors for taking them out for ice cream. Jacob, in anticipation of a new tree house, ran to the back to see what I had accomplished. I didn't see him. The saw was in full throttle and demanded my attention as it sliced through the horizontal branch.

"Dad! Dad!" Jacob yelled, but his voice fell short before the scream of the saw.

The branch was nearly down when the ladder unexpectedly shifted ever so slightly, but enough for me to reach out, taking my left hand off the hungry saw to balance myself against the tree. The next several moments were captured by individual snapshots frozen in my mind. In that split second, I found myself at the bottom of the tree. I have a memory of seeing my saw on the ground and me running up the hill. Another memory was seeing my son, Jacob, at the top of the hill by the garage. These moments would forever be engrained in my memory. I wasn't sure how much Jacob had seen, but he had taken off running as fast as a seven-year-old could run.

Screaming back to his mom, who was still talking to the neighbors, Jacob yelled, "Dad needs help!"

Seeing the panic in his face, Tracy knew something had gone terribly wrong. She sprinted up the driveway, not knowing what she would find. The neighbor followed, grabbing the kids along the way and instructing them to get back in the van. Tracy turned the corner at the back of the house, our eyes met, and all she saw was her husband of twelve years holding his arm to his chest. She couldn't tell what had happened, but a massive trauma was evident.

As our eyes met, I ripped the baby's blanket from her arms and wrapped it tightly around my arm. I shouted only one thing: "Honey, I'm in trouble!" The calmness in my voice was overshadowed by what was clearly a trauma to my arm.

The neighbor came around the side of the house and immediately instructed the kids, who were curious, to go back and sit in the van. Tracy, understandably panicked, rushed inside to call 911 as I instinctively kneeled and tucked my arm underneath both my knees to try and stop the bleeding.

Even though the world around me was in chaos, my world seemed to slow down to a crawl. I felt no pain, but my mind knew that it was in control, and a calm, precise spirit was all that was necessary.

As I sat hunched over, I heard Tracy scream, "No, you can't put me on hold!" The emergency hotline did put her on hold, and her panic increased twofold.

At that point, multiple people were trying to get emergency services there as quickly as possible. I was still calm, though I could feel my body changing rapidly. I felt a peace at that moment, even though I knew I was in serious trouble. I didn't have any idea of what damage had been done, but I felt that I needed to know. I slowly lifted my knees and unwound the blanket to see what was wrong.

Before I noticed that my arm would not turn or twist, I could see some damage to my hand. Quickly I rewrapped my arm and tried to rebalance myself with my knees on the wound. This awkward position forced me to hunch over and gave Tracy the impression that I had passed out, which only added to her panic. She finally connected with 911.

As my world continued to slow down, as if by design, I couldn't see the worse part of my arm. I still hadn't felt any fear or pain—just a calm awareness of what I needed to do in that moment. Somehow the mind has the power to separate all that's unnecessary and hold on to the thoughts needed to survive.

In an instant, things started to escalate; my mouth had become as dry as Death Valley. I yelled over my shoulder, "Tracy, I need water fast." This was my first moment of panic. I went so dry so quickly, I thought my throat was closing up.

As Tracy went over the details with the 911 operator, she quickly filled a glass and brought it out to me. I heard my wife's panic-stricken voice as she relayed information to 911. She let every emotion held inside her flood through the phone. "My husband has cut his arm off with a chainsaw, and he is bleeding to death. He needs help! Please get here now!"

Again, feeling my throat go terribly dry, I yelled back. "I have to have more water." For the second time, I felt panic creep into my head. Tracy, in a state of desperation, told the 911 operator, "I have to put the phone down to get him more water."

"No!" yelled the operator. "He is going into shock. Do not give him any fluids."

As Tracy relayed the information to me, my world suddenly sped up, and I knew my situation was changing rapidly. "Tracy, you need to come here. I can't hold myself up anymore." I knew that if I fell off my knees, there would be no control over the bleeding, yet I felt indescribably calm.

Then I had my first thought of not surviving. It wouldn't have taken long for the inevitable. Knowing emergency help was on the way, Tracy handed the phone off to the neighbor to communicate back and forth. Then she flew out the back door to cradle me. As if an angel in that moment knew she wasn't going to be able to steady me, a first responder showed up on scene. I looked up, in a stupor, and noticed that it was my old neighbor, Dee, who was on the volunteer fire department for Spring Arbor like her father.

Tracy immediately tried to compose herself and in a calming, reassuring voice said, "It's okay; they're here. Do you recognize who it is?"

I responded in a faint, exhausted voice, "It's Dee."

I began to go in and out of consciousness, so my perception of the scene was unclear. I wasn't sure when the rest of the people arrived, nor did I hear the constant flow of incoming sirens, but in one moment of clarity, I was on my back, and I looked up and saw Tracy standing at the corner of the house. Her face said it all: uncertainty.

"Tracy, you need to come down here with us," the neighbor said, trying to get her to go down to the van with the kids. The neighborhood had filled with emergency vehicles and a multitude of curious onlookers.

"I need to be here!" Tracy wept with uncertainty, comforted by a number of people surrounding the scene, including her cousin Bob, a first responder.

I had begun to show confusion. A large group of emergency people tried to stabilize me, flushing the wound with massive bottles of saline fluid, trying to clean out chain oil and wood chips. Others were cutting off my clothes and putting in an IV for fluids.

I didn't feel pain, but I would suddenly find myself screaming with incredible intensity as they flushed my arm with fluid. Incredibly, my mind, God, or a guardian angel had protected me from seeing how bad the injury was.

Volunteers kept the flood of curiosity seekers away as rumors pierced through the gathered crowd. And the chaos around me continued. My confusion seemed to have gotten worse.

Then my perspective of the accident suddenly changed; my view of the chaotic scene was from above. I was watching everyone work on the injured man who was screaming in pain, and the emergency techs were organizing ambulances and performing survival procedures. I could hear and see everything but with no clarity. It was as if the pain had become too much for my soul to bear, so it had separated from my body. I never felt dead, but this perspective removed me from the panic and offered security, as if I were watching a horror film on television.

The frantic scene included an EMT yelling down the driveway, "Get air evac, now!"

A minute later, they responded, "Not available!"

He told them, "We have to get advanced life support to the scene." Looking down at me, he said, "Bill, we have to wait for another ambulance to get here with advanced life support. You have to stay awake for me."

Tracy moved her head to listen to the EMT and then looked over to another first responder quizzically. "He is going to survive?" At this point, her tears restarted and began to flow uncontrollably.

I could see him talking, and it looked like I was responding in some obligatory fashion, but I wasn't there. I was fading away to somewhere else, like I was having an intense daydream as I fell asleep.

I felt an incredibly calming presence as I found myself in a beautiful but strange place. There was no pain, noise, or frantic movements. I was pretty sure I was still in the present moment, but I wasn't aware of time or the chaotic situation that I'd left behind. I can't even say I was aware of anything at all. The moments before seemed to vanish from my reality, but where was I and why was I there? Had I died?

Whether it was seconds or minutes later, I'm not sure, but I was surrounded by a profound glowing light—a light full of energy and in constant motion, flowing like a river full of spectacular colors.

2

A Walk through the Attic

*W*ith my strange sense of awareness changing, I seemed to have been removed from reality. Was this my new reality? Where did my life go, and would I see my family again? Or was this the beginning of my afterlife? This new reality seemed to be a sort of energy that filled me with calmness and security.

The horizon had no distance. I couldn't tell if it was within arm's reach or a hundred miles away. I had no feelings, regrets, or emotions whatsoever, as if I were part of a continuous energy with none of the differentiating factors that are a part of everyday life. Nothing had its own distinction of matter or emotion, just a spectacular hue of every color imaginable blending and yet flowing almost as perfect as a piece of precise artwork. Wherever I had been taken, it was surreal. This hue surrounded me and consumed every inch around me. My new universe was the energy of a light that flowed within itself.

As my mind worked its way through my new environment, cloudiness took over like an overcast day getting lost in a drifting fog. Everything in life with a physical characterization was gone. My thoughts seemed to react in sync with this new environment that consumed me. In fact, I seemed to be one with it as I flowed with its energy. Even though I thought there should be feelings of fear or desperation, I felt comfort and deep love flowing through me. I knew I was surely part of this energy.

As I looked around, I noticed that the horizon seemed to be taking form. The shapes were unrecognizable, but there was definitely something happening. It was almost like I was traveling closer, yet I didn't feel movement. As I turned again, there was a background as the horizon began to take shape. The magnificent hue surrounding me had changed colors and blended into a spectacular vision.

I turned to take in as much as possible. With no sense of direction, I focused on the developing background. Several flowing reds softened into a brilliant morning sunrise of yellows, oranges, and faint blues. The background seemed like a familiar place. It looked like a fair or carnival with steel structures and a Ferris wheel as the background came into focus.

I recognized the grandstand and knew it was the Jackson County Fair. The landscape continued to progress, and yes, there were Tracy and me. We were so young, definitely high school age. As I viewed the situation from a unique position, I realized I was indescribably part of the vision—so much so that if it were a painting, I wasn't in the painting: I *was* the painting. I couldn't interact but only observe, as if I were the caretaker of sorts.

With the smell of fresh fries, Italian sausage mixed with fresh onion, and peppers swirling in the air, we strolled through the midway, surrounded by the spinning steel rides and seemingly endless rows of food wagons. As their lights blinked and twinkled like a choreographed ballet of daylight stars, I knew it was a happy time in our life.

We made our way back to our favorite part of the fair. The aroma in the air was much different as we made our way back to the horse barns. We had always loved our horses. At that age, I'm not sure if we had ever talked about horses or our dreams, but we knew they'd brought us together. They, or we, seemed to be very happy.

As the vision seemed to come to fruition, I couldn't help but notice a change in me as I looked over the fair. I still had no emotional connection, but there was an overwhelming reaction that began swirling through me, as if I was supposed to see something. I wasn't sure what it was at that moment, but I knew the day had a special meaning.

As I started to ponder, something caught my eye, but when I turned, it was gone—in an instant. I was back in the air of peace and love that was filled with soft, flowing colors. They seemed to mix and flow like the changing light of the morning sunrise as the sky took on the flowing colors of the rainbow. This time there seemed to be pinker hues that flowed through the moment when I started to see shapes again.

A room started to form—not just any room, but one with equipment taking shape. A bed, monitors, and cabinets were filling the center of this vision, but what about—

It happened again before my thought was finished. It was Tracy in the bed with her mom on one side and my mother on the opposite side. I looked overwhelmed as I stood at the foot of the bed. Nurses started to fill the room like teammates in a huddle, waiting for the next play. It was the birth of our firstborn, January 4, 1986. I was still sixteen. It was a little scary at that time, but Tracy and I seemed to be at ease with little worry—or at least that's the way I remembered it. There was power with inexperience, no self-imposed fears or expectations.

The room continued to fill with people, and there seemed to be a bit of calm panic. Then a piece of the puzzle flowed through me as if I had been thrown right back into the chaos. Our baby had the umbilical cord wrapped around her neck, and the delivery was tenuous until she was out. At sixteen, I didn't understand or need to understand how bad the situation was at that moment.

Moments later, there she was, Ashley Brooke. As the doctor delivered her, the nurses swarmed like bees. My lack of reaction told me that, at that time, I didn't know the gravity of the situation.

I also didn't seem to notice that they whisked her off while clearing her mouth and lungs. Something appeared to be wrong as they continued to work on her and communicated with the doctor that she had a condition called beta strep from breathing in some meconium.

Tracy was exhausted, our moms were exalting, and I was overwhelmed and certainly happy that the delivery was over. I stood by the side of the bed with relief and in a quandary over what was next. The moment ceased.

Tracy and I had had a baby over Christmas break in our junior year of high school. The nurses returned with her. I, in the state of being the overseer of the scene, began to notice a change in the environment. The energy, or whatever I seemed to be a part of, melted the memory away, absorbing the colors back into a colorful river of energy.

I didn't feel confused but I could not grasp what the formation of colors was or if it was even real. It was like seeing Northern Lights—not only watching them but being part of them. My soul was somehow part of this magnificent show. I was flowing within the energy that I had come to call the Hue.

Now that the Hue was dominant again, no forms stood out. I was again part of this enlightened energy with flowing rivers of color. It had changed to a soft, embracing flow consisting of light yellows and shades of white. I thought, *It's like the lighting in a library or*— I couldn't even finish my thought. *This reminds me of the small chapel where*— And it happened again. I started to feel like this was a game or maybe there was something else at work.

I saw Tracy standing there in a beautiful white dress. She was so young, yet she stood there all in white as majestic as any bride could be. Age had no bearing on how beautiful she was as she stood there waiting to become one with her husband. As before, the vision was becoming focused, and details of that moment in time were forming. Tracy and I were getting married.

We stood atop the steps, and doubt was in everyone's mind but our own. The depiction of this memory seemed to be highlighted by the Hue. The dimly lit chapel seemed to focus on the two of us in brilliant white highlights. Everyone else sat there in the dark shades of doubt. We had just turned seventeen. The date was July 3, 1986. We were getting ready for our senior year in high school.

A bright light entered from the side of the chapel, and as I glanced over to see, it was over. "What is going on?" I queried out loud. "How can I get out of this dream? I have no control."

The Hue had taken over again, fading and blending into a magnificent blend of colors. It seemed to absorb and filter colors to create landscapes. The colors quickly put me at peace and settled my mind. Even though all this was absent of emotions, there was always a sense of security and peacefulness.

The Hue was different this time. It was darker. I didn't feel fear, but the surrounding colors set me back and certainly grabbed my attention. As the Hue around me turned to a mix of black and dark reds, I wasn't sure what form was taking shape, but by then I was sure I needed to look for something in my past.

Again, the immediate surroundings began to take shape. They were more difficult to pick out, because of the darkening Hue. There were lights, several different colored lights, blinking on and off in random patterns. I journeyed back through my memories, searching for some kind of connection.

"Maybe it's a UFO sighting!" I joked as my comfort level in the Hue increased and to bring back some resemblance of sanity. I saw infrastructure taking shape, and before I could form another thought, it hit me: I was in a nightclub. I didn't know where, but it was definitely a bar. I focused on trying to find meaning, and that wasn't easy when there were no feelings to help draw out memories.

Then, as if on cue, I saw myself at a much younger age, holding a beer and grooving to the music. I must have been in my early to mid-twenties, because I didn't drink or go to a bar until I was at least twenty-one. Just as I began to search for Tracy, another individual that I knew very well came into focus. It was my best friend, Patrick. He and I had become closer after high school and had developed a very trusting relationship.

I started to realize that before I could finish thinking a question about any moment before me, the answer was present. This furthered my curiosity about the Hue's existence. *Is my mind in control of the Hue? Am I actually the Hue?* I began to struggle, even among the loving feeling that I was surrounded by. I just couldn't help feeling that I was missing something. *Are these moments in time? Is my life passing before me? Am I supposed to gain insight?* As I searched for meaning, the Hue suddenly brightened. Not noticing the connection yet, I turned, only to find myself fading out of one memory and back into the magnificent calming energy all over again.

I couldn't help but wonder, *Why the bar scene? What's the connection with the other memories that had been shown to me?* The memories seemed to have nothing in common. I knew at that moment that I needed to look deeper.

This time, the Hue was altogether different. There was an intense energy that felt and appeared to be greater than any of the others before it. It was almost overwhelming, yet it steadied my spirit to my core. A path started to form, surrounded by lush grassy plains. The rivers of colors formed beautiful flowers flowing in a soft breeze filled with luscious fragrances.

As the Hue in the air seemed to lighten into a mesmerizing blue, the flowers continued to form with the mixture of all the other colors, as if they absorbed the Hue itself. It was truly a moment of grandeur, a deeper profoundness than any of my previous visions.

The path was rocky in some spots and well-traveled in others. The energy felt like it was walking me down the path. I seemed to be flowing within the spirit of the fantasy. I couldn't form any thoughts. It was like the majestic depths of the ocean, the impervious stance of Yosemite National Park, and the freshness of crisp winter air all beaming at the height of their lifecycle. It was magnificent.

This place was so different from my own memories that I couldn't help but cry out, "Is this what life is supposed to feel like? Have my thoughts been so egocentric that I missed all of this beauty that surrounds me? Or—is this heaven?"

I wasn't sure who I was yelling out to, but it was my first attempt to interact with my surroundings. I waited for a familiar place or person to show up, but only a continuous path led through the most spectacular setting I have ever witnessed. As I searched deep into the horizon, there seemed to be shadows that were out of focus. No matter how hard I tried to rein them in, they remained distant and unformed.

An intense pressure began to form around me. I looked around almost frantically to see what was approaching, but there was nothing but lush gardens filled with love and hope. Before I could start to make sense of the situation, a pressure surrounded me, and an incredible energy transferring into me.

"It's a hug!" I yelled out impulsively. This was the second time that I was compelled to interact with my environment. I never felt the need to question, just observe. As impulsively as I had yelled out moments before, I repeated myself, but this time with an inquisitive tone. "It's a hug, right?"

No response was needed. My heart opened, and the energy flowed into me as endless as the gorgeous fields that surrounded me. Even though I couldn't remember the last time I prayed, I was suddenly consumed with an outpouring of words. "Lord, I'm not sure where I am, and I'm certainly feeling confused with the lack of emotions and overthinking that typically controls my life. I don't feel like I need help, yet I ask for it. I don't recognize what is happening around me, yet I feel as if I am familiar. Even though my feelings are absent, I'm consumed by bewildering thoughts. Lord, this doesn't feel like a dream. Am I dead? Lord, please give me guidance. Amen." As I ended my prayer, the landscape changed again.

As randomly as the prayer was spoken, it just felt right. No explanation was needed. Wherever I was, I felt at home even in solitude.

I still had no concept of time. It hadn't even entered my mind, but I couldn't help but wonder if minutes had passed or days or maybe weeks. Wherever I was, it was timeless.

"What now?" I thought aloud as the surroundings began to fade. What seemed to be seconds after it had formed, I requested, "Don't leave this place. I am at peace."

I quickly turned to take in one last glimpse of that fantastic environment. As the warmth and energy that I recognized as a hug started to fade, the landscape vanished, and it was all gradually absorbed again by the mystical Hue. I started to process what had just happened and began to question this abstract entity that I was one with. *Is this part of my conscience or a dream? Is it heaven?*

As I put my thoughts together, warmth surrounded me again; the energy was changing. As I convinced myself that all of this was some intense part of my imagination, there was still one thing I could not understand. The energy had no emotional baggage. There weren't any feelings associated with it. It wasn't better than me, and I wasn't better than it. There wasn't a need to control or compete with it. But before I could get too caught up in thought, a horizon began to form all over again.

"Well, this is familiar," I thought aloud as the background quickly formed back into the fairgrounds. "What do the fairgrounds have to do with anything?" I quietly mumbled to myself. I realized that I was now communicating aloud. Whether with myself or with the Hue, I wasn't sure.

Thinking that this must have been a key moment in my life, I searched for recollection of that time. An emotion entered my mind for the first time since I had been caught up in this force of visions and energy. Although I felt relief or acceptance of some kind, there were different emotions mixed together, including fear. The fear felt like it was the underlying emotion, but at that moment acceptance dampened the strength of fear.

"Aha!" I yelled as I raised my arms straight up into the flowing colors. That day walking through the fair was a day of acceptance. "Yes, that was the day that Tracy and I drove to Lansing," I proclaimed aloud. "We went to a clinic to listen to our options and even possibly get the pregnancy aborted."

I started to remember the sense of calm that we both had that day. It seemed like it should have been a day filled with panic and fear, yet we accepted that we were going to be parents. We went to the fair after we found out Tracy was too many weeks along. That was our first blessing.

I mumbled, "Is acceptance what I'm supposed to see?"

As I searched intently, I watched us holding hands as if we were supporting each other against the world. Emotions from that day started to flood the Hue's environment. They had been held out of the earlier trip down memory lane, but now they took over, adding further details to that day and how overwhelming it could have been. Maybe it *was* that overwhelming; maybe God surrounded us with calm as part of his plan.

An abundance of thoughts began to flood my mind, firing off like popcorn popping in my head. I suddenly found myself feeling panicked, and as quickly as it started, a controlled calm returned to the Hue. The emotions had vanished, taking all my panicked thoughts with them as if the Hue took away the growing insecurities to refocus me on whatever task was at hand.

I took a moment and realized that as soon as life became too much, calmness was given to me. I looked deeper into that time of my life and began to put it together with the other visions. This only added to my confusion, and the overanalyzing began. "Too much too soon!" I hollered. I shook my head in confusion as I mumbled back to myself. "Who am I yelling at?"

I impulsively yelled out again. "How am I supposed to learn

anything?" A hospital room formed right in front of me again, similar to a mirage in the desert.

"Okay, if the fair was acceptance, what am I supposed to see here?" I said aloud with a bit of frustration.

The situation, at that moment, grew to one of despair. I knew there was a message, but I started to get impatient, and the Hue seemed to react to my state of mind. Was I controlling the Hue, or was it guiding me? The Hue's energy embraced me, and my thoughts once again became focused and centered.

I began to ramble through my thoughts, "The fair, the birth, the wedding. The fair, the birth, the wedding—the bar? What am I missing?"

As I viewed the birth again, it didn't seem like acceptance. It just didn't feel right. I knew that I had accepted the baby, but that was just too simple. Maybe it was the fact that I was there. I was actually in the room, at age sixteen, for the delivery.

I had accepted the relationship with the Hue when I asked, "Does this have anything to do with the challenges in life?" I didn't really expect a verbal response.

I waited patiently as the room again faded quickly into the chapel. I felt that I was gaining understanding, at least a little bit. The memories were coming in quicker, maybe because of my acceptance of the situation, even though I had no understanding of what or why this was happening. I still wasn't sure if this was my life flashing before my eyes or if I had already died. The wedding again formed right in front of me. Was this just another form of acceptance?

———

I had come home from Michigan State football camp four days before the wedding. That was an interesting year at camp. The coaches were talking to me and evaluating me in ways they hadn't in the past. They told me that they would get ahold of my high school coach and get some film of my games.

When the defensive coach spoke to me about going to Michigan State to play ball, I opened up about my having a child. He suggested that I talk with another player, who also had a child, about how he balanced family, school, and the game. I was aware of the other player's situation, and he didn't live with his child.

I had an intense love for my baby girl. This tore my heart because I really loved my family, even though Tracy and I weren't married yet. An intense fear entered my heart. This fear came from putting all of my energy into a sport that I loved and not having enough time for my family.

Walking into my house, I felt an all-time high over the possibility of playing ball for Michigan State, and I had come back to reality. I put my gear down, walked into the kitchen, and I saw my mother, Tracy's stepmother, and my sister sitting at the breakfast bar, talking. I wasn't sure I had seen the three of them together ever before. It was unusual, for sure, but I was on such a high from football camp, I didn't question it.

Before I could say much of anything, my mother threw me a curve ball by asking, "Do you want to get married?"

Although I was shocked at the timing of the question, after a short pause, I quickly responded, "Yes!"

As far as I was concerned, there wasn't anything to think about. This may have been naive, but Tracy and I spent every waking moment together with baby Ashley. I knew at age sixteen that I loved her and Ashley more than anything else in the world. Whether it was inexperience or God's plan, I knew it was right.

———

So, was it acceptance? Maybe, but it felt bigger than that. As warm emotions started to fill my heart, the world around me faded back into the familiar Hue. As its energy flowed around me like a rowboat being consumed by a massive ocean, the nightclub began to take shape.

This was where confusion took over my thoughts. *How could all of these situations be connected? What am I supposed to gain from the bar?* As I was doused in darkness, I pressed myself for answers to my thoughts. I was convinced that I had not died; instead, the Hue was trying to illustrate a lesson. I must have been standing too close to the tree and unable to see the forest surrounding me.

As I pressed and tugged for answers, memories flowed. I remembered the times. Patrick and I had spent a lot of time at bars—too much time. We would go to Canada's casino, Grand Rapids, for live music and to Battle Creek to a hip dance club. Typically we never got in trouble, but we certainly got in situations where we didn't belong, especially without our wives.

I cried out almost instinctively, "Lord, I know there is something here for me. Please guide me. I want to get this right."

As I finished, a vision within the vision came into focus. It was Tracy, sitting at home with two of our children, Ashley and Jacob. Jacob appeared to be around one and Ashley around six. This side scene brought on strong emotions. Though emotions or lack of them in these visions seemed to be controlled, that wasn't the case at that moment. I viewed a part of the vision with happiness and feelings of recklessness and having a good time. When I focused in on Tracy and the kids, the emotion turned to sadness and fear.

I became inundated with grief and guilt, and tears began to flow. This consumed every cell in my body. It was so painful that I tried to pull myself from the vision. What I needed to see in the situation was my lack of—what?

I buried my head in my hands to remove the vision from my sight, but the scene filled my conscience. "What? What connection am I missing?" I wrapped my hands around my temples as I glanced back into the vision.

Assuming that I was with God, I prayed, "Lord, I am seeing and feeling what you put in front of me, and I certainly did not act in a thoughtful or loving way to my family during that time. I ask for forgiveness. Please fill me with love and remove this guilt from my conscience." I was then immersed with remorse.

The vision went unchanged. I thought aloud, "I need to put this together. If this was supposed to be a lesson in life, I accepted the circumstances, I committed myself, but then I also lacked commitment."

As the emotions started to subside, I couldn't help but think about the last vision and its importance. My mind faded to the heavens like the past vision with a surreal setting. What did that vision mean? I reviewed in my mind a winding path, beautiful gardens, and a horizon that would not come into focus. As I pondered back and forth, I wondered if the path was my life and the lack of focus was the unknown future.

"Am I right?" I yelled out into the void of the vision, still picturing the bar and Tracy sitting alone at home. "Am I accepting certain situations in my life, both good and bad?"

Nothing. I noticed not a single change in the Hue. Whatever I was supposed to see was there, right then in that moment. Then suddenly my mind was filled with a quotation. The energy of the Hue flowed with words. "For whoever has will be given more, and they will have abundance. Whoever does not have, even what they have will be taken from them" (Matthew 25:29 NIV).

I tried to piece the puzzle together, which led to more questions rather than the answer I was searching for. This quote continued to flow through my mind. My Bible recollection was fuzzy, but the intense energy led me to believe Jesus said those words.

"Jesus?" I yelled out with an excitement. "Jesus was teaching about accountability? Is this about being accountable for what you have been given in life? The word is *accountability*! My lesson is accountability?"

At a very young age, my parents taught me that I had to be accountable for my own actions, and somewhere down the line I must have lost the edge of holding myself accountable. Had I become so unaccountable to myself, Tracy, and my kids that my future in the vision of the path remained unfocused? Had I lost my accountability? Was I going to lose what I cherished in life?

In my head, I ran through the visions over and over again. I felt the energy of accomplishment, yet it also felt like it was only the beginning. This set of visions with no emotions running through the energy taught me to be an observer, not a person who just watches life.

In a split second, I found myself back in the chaos, lying in my driveway, screaming because of the acute pain.

"Bill! Bill! You need to stay with us here." The paramedic was yelling in my face. "You have to stay awake!"

A second paramedic looked over at an ambulance driver. "We have to get him stable before we can move him."

As my sudden awareness of the accident settled back in, I faded in and out of consciousness. Intense pain radiated through my body as the large group of emergency personnel continued to flood my arm with saline solution. I was in a very different world than I had been in just moments before.

Tracy was still standing her ground at the corner of the house, trying to maintain some sort of composure. Commotion and chaos surrounded me again, and my confusion about where I had just come from grew into a vocalization as I began to mumble about the flowing light.

"Bill, the lights are coming from the emergency vehicles," the EMT said to keep me engaged in conversation. "Let's keep you here with us, and stay awake."

3

Vision of One's Self

*B*efore I knew it, my soul seemed to remove itself from the overwhelming pain, and I again found myself hovering above the chaos. The situation was getting more intense as they focused on trying to keep me alive while keeping my arm intact. Mostly volunteers at the scene, they helped vigorously, offering any assistance they could. Some had never seen such a gruesome accident, and they chose to help with crowd and traffic control. Even with this unique view, I still had not or could not see the extent of the damage to my left arm.

As another ambulance was approaching, a paramedic yelled down the driveway, "Make sure this one is advanced li—"

I had slipped away. As the Hue became my world, I anticipated peace. It wasn't as if I had a choice; I felt a willingness to go. I found myself immersed back in the security of the Hue. The flow of magnificent color and energy was back.

I wasn't sure if the Hue was God, but for the first time I started to consider the possibility that I was with God and maybe I was dying. So these visits were my penance, and then I would be accepted or denied entrance into heaven. With a remote chance of the past interaction being with God, the same random questions began to fill my mind. Was God prepping me for the afterlife? Was I already dead? With questions barreling through my head, everything stopped when the Hue surrounded me with a sudden calmness. There were no thoughts, just an unexplainable sense of calm that was so demanding that all thinking ceased immediately. It brought a welcome calm over me.

I settled in and looked in an upward direction. "Are you God?" With no visible response, I kept up my questioning, "Is this heaven?"

Again, there was no response that I could see or hear, but there was a difference in the Hue itself. Within that incredible flow of color and energy appeared a cloud-like entity. It was translucent in areas and as thick as pea soup in others. Like the Hue, it seemed to flow with its own energy. But it filled only a small area of the Hue's brilliance. I couldn't recollect if this was there the first visit or not.

The cloud appeared to be a separate entity. In fact, it moved independently throughout the Hue. It filled minimal space, and as with the Hue, I could not tell its boundaries. I wasn't sure if it was one foot in front of me or a hundred miles away. I had convinced myself that this misty cloud had not been there the first time. It stood out like a single storm cloud against a clear blue sky. The mist didn't seem to interrupt the energy of the Hue as it flowed through me with a loving comfort as it always had. Just as I began to focus more thought into solving this new piece of the puzzle, my eyes were caught by something forming in the background.

Rubbing my hands together eagerly, I redirected my focus. "Here we go, something from my past. I hope this will clear up this new mystery of the mist."

This time around, I was beaming with confidence because I knew I would be ready to solve the riddle given to me through visions of my past. As the Hue blended and transformed into the scenery, giving it form, I noticed emotions immediately as the view came into focus. This set me back, because my emotions had been mostly controlled in my last visit.

The vision that came into focus was my parents' home, in which I had never lived as a child. Tracy and I had been married for two years when they moved into it. As I began to think of memorable moments that would have come from that period of time, an overwhelming feeling of anger swept through the Hue. It was painful, and it was followed by regret.

The vision continued to develop, with my brother and sister standing in the kitchen. In milliseconds, I was scanning my mind. So much emotion charged the energy of the Hue that I felt myself pull back as if I were trying to remove myself from that unrecognizable moment. The Hue surrounded me with safety and love, yet there I sat, with too much emotion to bear in that one moment of time, as if I was getting ready to experience something horrible all over again.

I reached my hands around the back of my head, and my elbows created a tunnel so I could focus all of my attention on the developing scene. "I'm supposed to be accountable for something here, right?"

Then it happened, my brother and I were in a physical fight. My size and strength took over very quickly as I pinned him to the floor. The emotions didn't just flow through the Hue; they fired off like high-energy lightning bolts, and they were ugly. Pain and anger seemed to overtake the loving energy of the Hue. The fight didn't last long, but a bitterness hovered in the vision. There had been so many emotions crammed into one short moment as I watched the scene unfold.

I sat there trying to collect my thoughts. There was nothing— no thoughts about what the fight was about or who said what to start it. Why was there so much negative energy about nothing?

As the emotions began to settle, I hadn't even noticed that the mist shrouded the entire vision in darkness, leaving very little Hue in the periphery. The raw emotions began to fade as the Hue again absorbed the background and returned to its fluctuating brilliance.

"Accountability, right? I'm supposed to be accountable for my actions?" I asked softly as the question was driven out of me through an emotional impatience created by the intense interaction. Either way, I was relieved it was over.

The Hue firmly took over again, and the mist appeared defiant, even as its mass and color faded. The strength and magnificence of colors seemed to pull energy out of the misty cloud. It softened back to a transparent white and decreased in size significantly. Because I had no reference for size or distance, I estimated that it was at least a quarter of the size it had been during the vision and still shrinking.

As things started to calm down, an experience started within the Hue's energy. This time was altogether different. I didn't see forms but blocks of words, like precise mental visions. Phrases started to run through and around me. Sentence fragments flowed through the energy like bubbles racing down a rapid river. They were part of the energy but altogether separate. The mist was also changing in and out, from shades of white to the blackest of black. The mist seemed to be flowing with what I assumed were random thoughts. I began to experience extreme confusion, just disconnected thoughts firing off randomly. "I wish that I would have—I should have—next time I will—I was so angry—if that person—I can't believe this. Why me?" These thoughts ran wildly through the Hue as the mist again grew. Anger and regret were among the emotions connected with certain phrases. They would hit me as if I was experiencing certain chaotic moments in life—moments that were not connected to any sense of time or an individual memory. They were just random wasted thoughts that created powerful emotions.

My face felt like it was showing the wear of confusion. "But what moment am I supposed to see? Is this one moment or several?" I asked aloud as the chaos intensified to the point where I closed my eyes and tried to gather myself.

There was no escape; the powerful energy was racing through

me, creating panic, self-pity, anger, and arrogance. Just as I began to feel helplessness, it was gone. It was as if someone had turned off the switch. For the first time since being in the Hue, I felt helpless and overwhelmed. I no longer felt the love or security flowing through the Hue. Moments before, I had been confident in my return to the Hue. I now felt small, out of control, and lost.

Like previous experiences in the Hue, there was a response as those thoughts began to form in my mind. The Hue was working its magic. I went from helplessness to intensely secure again. I felt the love surround me as if it had never left. As the emotions subsided, the mist shrank to almost nothing. It was clearly much smaller and lighter in color than it had ever been. I acknowledged the mist's existence, and I gathered myself.

As I tried to get my bearings, my thoughts began to fire rapidly, similar to the experience I'd just gone through. What was I supposed to see? Why was the experience so overwhelming? There was no physical world, just thoughts. How could simple thoughts create such an overwhelming state of mind? Why did the mist grow so large and dark with the intensity of emotions? Random problem solving continued to run through my head.

With a moment to relieve the building pressure, I rested my forehead on my fingertips, looking down as if the weight of all the thoughts had become too heavy to keep my head up. "God, if you are God, I recognize my past failures to be accountable, but this feels like it's more than accountability. What am I missing? Please show me a path to resolution!" And with that, the Hue's colors were being absorbed into another background.

I took a deep breath from exhaustion. "Now what?!" With that exclamation, the mist turned dark and began to increase rapidly in size. Noticing this immediate change, I realized that the mist might be reacting to me.

With a quizzical look, I asked, "Am I in control of this mist?" and with a bit of sarcasm, "How is this a lesson?" Clearly my confidence had withered.

The mist continued to darken and grow beyond the limits I had previously known. It had grown so dark that it blocked out parts of the Hue's shapes forming in the background. In some strange way, it began to give me a sense of identity, a sense of self that didn't seem to exist inside the Hue. In a moment of clarity, I recognized the selfishness I had begun to exert on the Hue's energy. My confidence and control had grown into a blanket covering everything that represented truth.

With that recognition, the mist began to recede, and the tension I felt was being relieved. It had greatly reduced in size and revealed that the Hue had still been forming a new horizon while that moment of self-indulgence seemed to consume the space further, indicating that these were two separate entities. Even though the shaded mist had lightened in color, I felt I needed to hold tight to this self-imposed control.

"Why or how does the Hue continue to work behind the scenes?" I blurted out. I wasn't even sure if it was a question or an observation.

The background took shape and was similar to the nightclub scene that I experienced in my last visit. As the Hue blended itself into the background, it seemed to be a collage of darkness. Nightclubs and opaque views continued to form like the random thoughts in the vision before it. The vision brought heaviness with it, shrouded with guilt and selfishness. The drain on the energy around me was clear. I was hanging in a cloud of self-pity and doubt.

The mist gained strength again, highlighting my pretentious visions with darkness. I had once again become very uncomfortable within the Hue's energy. I assumed the random backgrounds of bars and shady situations were places I had visited. Although some of the times it looked fun, the overwhelming feeling was despair and loneliness.

I wanted to yell in frustration, but instead, as if the Hue knew I'd had enough, a sense of humility flooded over me like a fresh blanket of white snow. For the first time since I had returned to the Hue, I started to see what I was supposed to understand.

Before I could ask my next question, the Hue absorbed the background and returned to its own magnificence. I was immediately warmed by the sense of an embracing hug. After such desperation and darkness, the rich colors of the Hue brought peace and removed my insecurities.

The relief swelled my emotions as my eyes watered. I began to explore my thoughts for meaning, and I noticed that the mist had dissipated back into a soft, transparent cloud. I was at peace, and my mind had settled in the moment.

As if I were getting too comfortable, the Hue was at work again. This time it brought a much brighter vision. The colors blended back into the never-ending road. The flowers again absorbed the magnificent colors of the Hue, and unclear forms sat off in the distance. This vision was filled with love and passion. Extraordinary views portrayed everything good in life, from the soft, flowing fields rippling in the breeze to the majestic mountains reaching to the height of the Hue's vision. The path where I was standing was filled with jagged stones and uneven footings. I took it all in, but I couldn't help but notice that I was surrounded by beauty and peacefulness, yet there I stood upon the most treacherous part of the path. The Hue, as if it sensed my desperate thoughts, embraced me with another thought-provoking quote: "For now we see only a reflection as in a mirror; then we shall see face to face. Now I know in part; then I shall know fully, even as I as fully known" (1 Corinthians 13:12 NIV).

The source of this quote was unknown to me, but the sense was that it came from an enlightened individual. I reflected back on the visions and the chaos from which I had just come. My mind seemed to be stuck in chaos, creating tension and pain while I stood on the jagged path.

As if not to dwell too long in one spot, the Hue began to absorb the surreal surroundings, quickly returning to the flow of energy and color. It wasted no time before returning me to my parents' home. The feelings of the moment seemed different this time. They were softer; there was still pain and anger, but it wasn't as intense. The softer emotions allowed me to search deeper, and I noticed that there were more emotions than I first realized. The personal pain, envy, and despair seemed to be intertwined with a need for growth, recognition, and love.

All of these emotions collided at once and seemed to fuel the moment. There were young egos looking for differentiation. No matter what it was, my brother and I didn't have the tools to deal with all the emotions that filled that room, so we reverted back to childlike behavior, creating more chaos and pain. As this vision continued longer than the last time, I realized how deep the emotions were buried inside me. I had clearly held these feelings until they erupted like a volcano.

Random emotions continued to fly through the vision as they had in the previous encounter. A need for acknowledgment, stemming from rejection and fear, had spiraled out of control. Maybe it was a sense of rejection coming from my parents. I don't know if it was disappointment or embarrassment because their son had a baby and was married so young.

Because I was so focused on looking into that moment of history, I failed to realize that the mist had grown extensively, taking over most of the background and darkening the scene as if it was reacting to the emotional event that transpired. As the emotions continued to grow, I started to realize that maybe these feelings, at least in part, were self-inflicted.

Was this the treacherous path from the previous vision? I began to contemplate choices that I had made. What lesson was the Hue trying to illustrate for me? Was I choosing to feel negative? What was I gaining from it? Was this about choices I made in the past?

As I started to explore that possibility, the Hue quickly brought on a flood of random thoughts. It seemed to be an easy transition, since the emotions were flying vigorously through me already, creating a vast array of random thoughts and questions. My concern immediately became whether I would be able to make it through the intense energy again.

"What do random chaotic thoughts have to do with choices?" I asked out loud as I felt nervousness building inside me. As I observed my surroundings in that moment, I noticed that not only were the chaotic feelings dampened as they swirled through the Hue, but the mist was noticeably lighter in color.

I brought my right hand to my chin as if to intensify my thoughts. "It's deeper than choices. It's—"

The background suddenly came into focus out of the depths of darkness. I was back to the collage of bars. This collage of memories was the most confusing. My mixed emotions wrapped these visions tightly with darkness. I could feel my absence in my family's life. I couldn't explain it, but it was a loneliness sent through the Hue's energy right to the center of my now heavy heart. My head and shoulders dropped simultaneously as an unsolicited feeling of guilt shaded my view. "This is about choices. It is about me making selfish decisions."

On cue, before I could get my thought completely out, the Hue had taken me back to the path, which was surrounded by the most picturesque landscape of color and nature that I had ever seen. It seemed to be more brilliant than ever before. *Maybe this is the path of life*, I thought. Surrounded by love, peace, and tranquility, I noticed sharp pains moving upward from my feet. As I looked around, I noticed that I was still standing on the rocky part of the pathway. Even though I was experiencing tremendous pain and discomfort, I remained there on the path. I was standing in the middle of heaven on earth, yet I could focus only on the pain I was feeling.

"Why do I stand here in this spot, right here, right now?" Shaking my head in confusion seemed to provoke more questions than answers.

Something was keeping me there on the path. Had I convinced myself that my life was so good that I no longer noticed the pain? Had it just become a normal part of life? As I searched the pathway, I noticed that if I continued to go in that direction, the path became more treacherous, but just a step away was a path down the center of lush green grass and sweet-smelling fields of beautiful flowers.

I realized in that moment that it was a choice to be there in pain and despair. It was my decision to dismiss the calls to change direction. The farther down that path I went, the heavier the pain would become. Yet I chose not to step out of a comfort zone, even in the midst of pain. I chose to stay right where I was, in an unacknowledged and accepted misery. The decisions that I made before had led me to that exact spot. If I continued to make similar decisions, the road didn't get better, but much, much worse. My lack of perspective or—

"Yes!" I looked to the sky and with exuberance shouted, "Awareness!" A sense of relief flowed through me as I realized that was the answer to the taxing and emotional ride.

I had become so unaware of myself, my thoughts, and the hypothetical realities that I was standing in self-pity and a self-created chaos. I had lost self-awareness only to drown in a false sense of security. My world had been about the greatness of my own self-created reality.

I cried out, "Lord, please guide me and give me a new self-awareness in every moment. Lord, give me the energy and wisdom to embrace each moment and to see myself where I stand."

The mist, which I hadn't realized was there, became nearly transparent. The Hue began to absorb the landscape, soaking in all of its magnificence. With all of its glory, I began to think about—

"Bill, Bill, you need to stay with us here," the EMT yelled as he leaned directly in my face. "I need you to stay focused here—right here, right now."

As a volunteer medic rushed the flat-board up the driveway, he screamed, "The advanced life support is here."

"We have to get him stable before we move him," a second EMT advised as the chaos continued.

I screamed out in pain as the emergency crew flushed the gaping wound. I tried to focus on my wife standing at the corner of the house. Our hearts connected through the depths of her tear-soaked eyes. I saw an undying love stricken with fear as her expression spoke an endless number of words.

4

Unforeseen Pain

*W*hat seemed to be a recurring theme happened again. I found myself viewing the accident from above. There was no pain. I just watched it as if I were a bystander at the scene of an accident. I still had no sense of time, so I wasn't sure how long it had been since I had come and gone from the Hue or even how long I had been lying on the driveway. By then, my comfort with the Hue gave me a sense that I was ready to return. The last time, intense emotions had surfaced, and the landscapes had been difficult enough not to ever want to go back. But I resolved that I needed to complete what had been started. The comfort of the Hue continued to fill me with an indescribable sense of security and love that made me feel at home. A need for resolution had sprouted from deep within my spirit. And with that, I was back within the comfort of the Hue's energy. Even though I had been there before, the exhilaration and intensity filled me with a childlike desire for life, hope, and direction. It was a thirst for life that I hadn't felt in some time.

My enthusiasm could not be contained as I yelled, "I'm ready! I'm ready to take on accountability and become more self-aware!"

As I sat there in a euphoric state of mind, I let go. There were no stressful random thoughts, no guilt from the past or worries about the future—just peace. The Hue's energy filled all of that empty space with love, peace, and hope all over again. It pushed out all remaining stress and mindless thinking. I was sure that I had never experienced harmony in my entire life like the Hue.

I settled in, just trying to soak it all up. "Is this how great life is supposed to feel? If this feeling is attainable and this is life's greatest feeling, I have missed the mark." Creativity filled the energy flowing through me like scenic rivers with constantly changing landscapes, colors, and smells. Love swirled like the colors on a tie-dye shirt, creating a never-before-experienced harmony. The intensity of energy was even greater than on my last visit. I was beginning to wonder if I wanted to go back home.

The Hue began to form its landscape, interrupting my last thought as it crossed my mind. I knew this place right away, but I wasn't sure of the situation. There seemed to be a collage of visions all over again. I saw me going to college, on my job, and in my manager's office. I was at Michigan State University, sitting in a large group. It looked like one of my advanced math classes. (I was studying to become a math teacher.)

In the next view, coming into focus toward the center of the vision, I was at work. It was the auto repair shop, and I was working second shift in the service department. My schedule ran from four thirty in the afternoon until two in the morning. Tracy worked days at the apartment complex, selling leases, and I was home with Ashley. When Tracy came home at four in the afternoon, I left for work. Three days a week I dropped off Ashley at daycare while I went to classes at Michigan State. The late evenings provided a slower time for me to get my homework done for my next day's classes. It was a crazy schedule, but it worked, and we finished what we needed to get done.

The third vision of the collage was my manager and I speaking in his office at the shop. I wasn't sure what we were talking about, but we often had conflicts about work versus family. That was different from my life with Tracy; we had been successful as a young couple because we took on challenges together. This conflict put enormous pressure on us when Ashley was sick and couldn't go to daycare. This added tension to our relationship.

As I looked closely at this conversation, my manager's usual intense professionalism stood out to me. I saw him as a hard-working, driven individual, but I also saw him as misguided when it came to family priorities. He did well for himself and worked extremely hard, but that didn't always transfer over to his family life. As I focused on the conversation, I was confused. There was happiness mixed with a sense of loss. The emotions flowing were coming from me, like I was gaining something but losing something important all at the same time.

"That's it! This was the conversation where he asked me to quit college," I hesitantly said aloud. As recognition filled my questioning mind, I hadn't even noticed the tension that took over my body, including my clenched fists. The hindsight of a poor decision still had a physiological effect on me.

The moment seized me right then and there as emotions began to fill the vision. They seemed hurtful and filled with regret as they flowed through the energy. He needed a trusted employee to run the service department at his second location. So he was going to pay me about half of what he paid the outgoing manager, because I didn't have enough experience or a college degree. A seemingly difficult decision was made easy as I remembered that the birth of our second child was coming. Even though I wouldn't be making the salary that the job should pay, it was much more than I had been earning. At that time of struggle in our lives, it made sense to make more money in the short run—or was the driving force of the grand feeling coming from the fact that my manager, whom I looked up to, wanted me? It was most likely both. I was in my third year of college, and it was intense and dragging. That moment with the employer was most likely the last thing I needed at that time in my life, but I was sick and tired of school.

As I searched through the visions, more emotions started to surround me like a heavy blanket. There was a fear of growing up in the unknown yet there was excitement that Tracy and I seemed to be making it through life, like we had finally grown up. I didn't differentiate that these were just public perceptions with no merit. I saw it as being an adult.

There was also a little underlying discontent flowing through the vision. I saw glimpses of dark red flash through, leaving a streak of anger. I assumed this was coming from a buried emotion because my employer had made me an offer or at least hung the carrot out in front of me. I assumed these emotions were attached to his stance that he wouldn't pay me as much because I didn't have a college degree, yet he had asked me to leave college. In my immaturity, I was not strong enough to keep a long-term focus in front of me.

As I thought back to my previous experiences with the Hue, I searched for answers. I could easily see accountability and self-awareness in this collage. My boss had dangled the carrot, but I was the one who had made the decision to let my dream of being a teacher go. I decided to take the immediate gratification, which seemed to be the easier path. Although accountability and self-awareness are both relevant here, it didn't feel right. I felt that the Hue had been taking me deeper and deeper with each visit, but I was missing something. The emotions running through the vision revealed that I was hanging on to past successes or failures instead of looking forward to life's new adventures.

Before I could get another thought out of my head, the Hue was soaking up the color from the visions, sending calm through my mind. In what felt like seconds, I realized I hadn't even noticed the mist. Was it there? Was I consumed by it? As I searched my visual memory of what I had just experienced, the Hue was wasting no time and was forming again.

My entire family was there. My manager had recently moved, and this vision was at his home. My boss, his wife, and their children hosted Tracy and me with our two kids, along with the two other managers and their families. It appeared to be Christmas. The living room was exploding with holiday decorations. His wife loved a trendy Christmas tree beautifully adorned with the latest fashionable decorations and ribbons. My boss had added a remote-control train around the bottom of the tree, as if the birth of his son gave him permission to go back to his childhood loves. With rows of hanging garland wrapped in golden ribbons, the smell of fresh cooked ham, green bean casserole, and baked rolls loomed in the air. As the smell of food swirled through the house, the Christmas party looked like it wouldn't disappoint.

My attention was directed away from the holiday spirit. The five of us—my boss, his wife, the two other managers, and me—were meeting in the sunroom. As usual, when the five of us got together, it was about politics and growing responsibilities at the workplace. Tracy and the kids were out in the living room, having hors d'oeuvres and hanging out with the other wives and children. Excitement filled the room as the kids hung out around the tree, scoping out the gifts.

As I viewed the vision, I couldn't hear the discussion, but the body language told the story. It was a scene that played out regularly. The emotions started to flood in again, confirming what I already knew. We were having some sort of discussion about business. The feelings that rushed in were disgust, sorrow, and even loneliness.

Why would I be feeling loneliness in that situation? With that thought, a bolt of anger flew through me. It literally pulled all of my attention away from the situation. It didn't last long, but it was piercing like an electrical shock. The emotions created tension; there were no signs of the joy of the holiday. Nobody, including me, seemed to be paying much attention to why we were there, except maybe the people in the other room.

As I started to feel the intensity rise in the sunroom, it was gone. The Hue had pulled all of the emotion away and absorbed the scene back into its own magnificence. I must say that when the visions gained a negative intensity, it was a great relief to be pulled back into the Hue.

I rubbed my head in confusion. "What am I supposed to see? I can't get enough in such a short time."

Again I was not expecting a response, but Hue seemed to react and began forming a vision that I had already experienced. It was my best friend, Patrick, and I hanging out at bars, enjoying music, dancing, and drinking. This vision was dark. The first time I saw this vision, I assumed it was dark because of the time of night. But this seemed different. Was it the mist?

As the Hue seemed to open a door of emotion, I felt something unusual. As with the vision of Christmas, there was pain and loneliness, but now there was also uncertainty, which flooded my body. It was so powerful that I had trouble coming to grips with it. I struggled to make a connection because it didn't seem to be related to this vision. With that short burst of emotion, it was gone. I was at rest again, flowing with the Hue as the remaining negativity floated away. It appeared that the Hue was presenting these visions with short emotional bursts so I didn't have time to overthink them.

I felt anxiety building, and I erupted impatiently with a question—this time with an expectation of getting an answer. "What am I supposed to be seeing? The emotions appear to be unrelated to the vision—or are they tied to someone else?"

It was a light-bulb moment. Maybe I wasn't seeing the entire vision. Maybe I had been so focused on the pain and myself that I had missed or didn't see another part of the vision. Again I didn't recall seeing the mist. Why wasn't it there? Was the mist the answer to this riddle? Had the mist blocked part of the vision? An endless number of questions raced through my head.

"Wait!" I called out loud. "The mist!" I continued to speak my broken thoughts into the Hue. "Is the mist altering my visions? Is the—"

The response was swift. There were no words, just a visit back to the path of life, as I had come to call it. This had become my favorite place to visit. The rich colors of nature filled my heart with peace, the embracing love in the air secured me to my core, and the sweet aroma put my mind at ease. The hopefulness grabbed me and took me for a ride through my biggest dreams.

As I looked around, enamored with the sheer beauty, I began to feel that familiar pain in my legs, generating from my feet. Even though I didn't seem to be standing on the stone path, the pain was intense. I must have gotten used to the pain being there, because my mind slowly moved back into the feeling of acceptance and ignored the signs of anything wrong. I noticed in the distant a couple of different backgrounds. Though they were both out of focus, I could tell they were clearly different—perhaps different choices in life.

"Do I have a life-altering decision coming?" I asked out loud, which seemed to be my new norm. I folded my hands in front of me as a calm energy flowed through me.

As quickly as it began, it was over. This was a place where I would have enjoyed spending more time, but the Hue worked with a purpose. While it returned to all its glory, it left me with more questions than answers. A thought swept into me as if it was put there on purpose: *The mist, what happened to the mist? Did I miss it again?* That was the question I dwelled on, because it seemed to be the answer. The Hue began to shape the collage of college, work, and my boss.

The question had become "Have I gotten so used to the mist that I failed to recognize its existence?" That question resonated throughout the Hue. That was the key to the next door in the Hue's life lesson.

Now fully immersed in the vision, I realized that the backgrounds were different in some way. I wasn't sure what had changed, but I was confident that they were indeed different. The emotions were more intense this time. I couldn't put my finger on it, but I had a gut feeling that something right in front of me had changed. I intensified my stare into the vision. Then, as if it was planted in my soul, the question of the mist swirled through my head as if it was all that mattered. I needed to take a broader look.

The vision looked the same. College classes, making ends meet despite crazy schedules, and the meeting with my boss were consistent with the previous visions, but the emotions had taken a noticeable turn. The excitement didn't seem to be generated from me taking a new position with the company. It was coming from a different direction. And as if that wasn't enough, loneliness and fear added to my confusion. The emotions had become intertwined like a push-pull effect.

"The mist—I am supposed to be searching for the mist." I felt restlessness begin to take over my body.

As I came back to center and looked intently for the mist, I noticed that the collage of visions didn't have an edge or a distinct border. There was no clarity. I began to consider that the mist had shrouded the vision and changed my view.

As I finished that thought, the Hue took over and quickly brought back into focus Christmas at my boss's home. Again the difference was a gut feeling but must have been too subtle for my eyes to catch. Maybe I had not learned enough about self-awareness yet to view the differences in these new visions. So I immediately searched for the mist.

Raising my hands in victory, I yelled with a sense of accomplishment, "I see it. I see the mist," hoping the Hue would take notice. It didn't take long before the mist was surrounding only the sunroom in which my boss, his wife, and his three managers, including me, were sitting. It nearly blocked out the entire living room, where Tracy, the kids, and the other families were sitting by themselves. Most likely, Tracy removed herself from the situation, because holidays were very special to her. They certainly were not about work; they were about coming together as a family, sharing our lives together with a little extra love.

As I recognized that the mist hadn't disappeared at all, I realized that it seemed to be connected to what and how I saw the vision. With that being said, I wasn't seeing the whole picture, and I was convinced that these seemingly disconnected emotions where coming from somewhere else. Were these emotions that I was dragging through life like a knapsack filled with sentimental value? Were they tied together from other life experiences? Was I having random chaotic thoughts in those moments that led to the disconnected emotions?

Deep down, I sensed that wasn't it. I had somehow missed the connection between the mist and the emotions. The Hue continued to cycle visions, wasting no time. I was quickly returned to the bar scenes with Patrick. I felt that if I was going to put this together, I had to get it right then. I felt that I was close, but I hadn't connected the dots with the emotions until they flooded back into the bar scene—and flood they did. With an incredible intensity, they filled my space. An unknown source of pain, loneliness, and uncertainty swarmed the vision. It created uneasiness inside me as I knew the mist was darkening the vision. The emotions took over and were so intense I defensively crossed my arms in front of me and bowed my head in humbled defiance. The emotions were screaming for attention as I looked intensely through the bar's lights. "What can't I see?" Frustration and impatience had a firm grasp.

"No!" With a sudden awareness, the tension released in my arms. "*Who* can't I see?" I unfolded my arms and refocused my attention.

As if God himself had rung my bell, it became apparent in an instant: these visions weren't about me at all; they were about Tracy. The disconnected feelings that rushed in were hers, not mine. The pain, loneliness, uncertainty, and anger were all her emotions trapped inside, waiting for me to acknowledge them. The mist had distorted my view and even blocked out the connection with

Tracy. The overlooked perception of self-awareness had created this lack of empathy.

As the puzzle started to divulge its secret, the Hue took me back to the path of life. I couldn't help but notice that it was different from the earlier visions. This time the pain coming up through my feet was much more intense. As I looked around, searching all of the magnificence that life had to offer, I envisioned myself standing in a plush path in the middle of my hopes and dreams.

The Hue, as if to acknowledge that I was not getting it, changed my point of view. I found myself looking down, overseeing the entire glorified path and all of the beauty in its serene landscapes. I quickly noticed that the pain I was feeling generated upward from my feet because I was standing on some of the roughest, most jagged rocks on the entire path.

But that wasn't all. From this vantage point, I could see that I was immersed in the darkest mist I had seen to this point. It shrouded me from every direction, and I hadn't recognized its presence. The mist had covered me for so long that I didn't or couldn't realize how it changed me and everything that I experienced. All I had to do was take one step in any direction, and it would have greatly changed my perspective. The pain that I had come to know and live with became part of my everyday outlook on life. I had accepted it as reality.

As I felt the elation of victory, I screamed, "My lack of perspective or empathy has led me to believe that everything is so good that I failed to see or listen to my truth!"

This statement sailed through the energy of the Hue as if it were being generated by the purity of nature's breeze itself: "Then we will no longer be infants, tossed back and forth by the waves, and blown here and there by every wind of teaching and by the cunning and craftiness of people in their deceitful scheming" (Ephesians 4:14).

Again I didn't hear words, but the visual in my mind was clear that this was the message. With a lack of awareness in the midst of no accountability, there was only one perspective. How could I miss so much in life by not noticing my lack of perspective? Perspective without the mist had opened up an entire new world.

"Aaahhhh!" I screamed as they rolled me over so they could slide the backboard under me and cinch a neck collar in place. My return to reality left no doubt that I was still alive. I wasn't sure how fast I was traveling back and forth, but when I was in the Hue, it felt timeless.

"Bill, we are going to get you loaded up soon. Keep your arm right here with no movement!" The lead EMT gave me instructions as he carefully secured my arm to my stomach area. "I have administered the maximum amount of morphine that I can give you. Just stay awake, and stay here with us! I need you to keep talking with me, not the light."

The volunteers worked feverishly to clear a path down the driveway, which had been overtaken by curious neighbors.

"Tracy?" I asked in an exhausted haze.

"Bill, are you still with us?" the assisting EMT said while working to keep my attention. "Your wife is going to ride in the front seat of the ambulance with us to the hospital."

Even in the fogginess of the moment, I heard Tracy's shaky but reassuring voice. "Billy, the neighbors have the kids, and my parents are meeting us at the hospital. Everything is going to be okay." With a slight squeeze of my hand, her energy reassured my heart. "I love you!"

5

The Riddle of the Mist

*S*eemingly instantaneously after "I love you," I saw the entire street from above. The neighborhood was filled with two ambulances, several volunteer fire trucks, and too many people to count. Fairway Drive, normally a quiet little neighborhood, now looked more like it was hosting a Fourth of July parade. There were lights from one end to the other as crowds of neighbors and ambulance chasers looked on in curiosity. This snapshot haunted me, because my perspective seemed to follow the gurney down the driveway. With a view from above, I stood on a mountaintop, looking down on the entire street. Without warning, I slipped away to the Hue.

Still without any way to gauge the amount of time that had gone by since my last visit, I felt as if I had never left. Love quickly filled my space, calming me after the chaos of reality. My mind settled and began to ponder what was next as the Hue swallowed me up in its wonder. As I reflected on past visits, I anticipated the next lesson. If the trend stayed the same, this lesson would require me to go much deeper than before; I knew intense emotions would likely follow.

Briskly rubbing my hands together with nervousness, I confidently anticipated whatever was coming. "Let's get learning!"

The Hue didn't seem to react in the usual fashion. A calm energy still ran through me from its embracing environment, but a landscape in the horizon never formed. After what seemed to be several minutes, anxiety started to build. I couldn't recall the Hue reacting that slowly in the past. I searched through my recent lessons again, hoping to find something I had missed.

As I threw my hands up in the air, I impatiently asked, "What is going on here? Why is there nothing happening?" I continued to yell questions as my impatience grew, ending with, "Have I learned all the lessons you have to give?" My confidence inside the Hue had become arrogance. I felt at ease with the Hue, which had made me overconfident.

Maybe the lesson I needed to learn was to be of a calm mind. With no sense of how long this had been going on, I started to search the Hue. At first, I didn't notice anything different. Everything inside it seemed to flow the way it always had in the past. Although the colors weren't as brilliant as during previous visits, they carried the same love and calming spirit.

I repeated my questions out loud. "Have I learned everything? Is this the end?" Then I paused and asked, "Now what am I supposed to do?" As I continued to question the Hue and myself, I searched deeper into my experiences.

Accountability, self-awareness, and being able to see and feel different perspectives all were lessons from the past. These lessons seemed to overlap and work within each other. Living life in the moment was certainly at the forefront. I sat in the middle of the Hue, feeling its energy of love secure me from the reality of the accident that I seemed to have left in a different dimension of sorts. I still wasn't convinced that it wasn't some sort of dream. The thoughts of lessons past started to seep through the Hue as they choreographed with the flow of color. There were no horizons or landscapes, yet I began to feel insecure. The Hue continued to lose its dynamic luster. I felt frustration, and panic settle in throughout my surroundings. This was unusual because any time that I'd had this type of emotion, it was part of a vision. My feelings and a darkness that appeared to be overtaking the Hue filled my thoughts with anxiety.

"What is going on? Why is this happening? Help me see what I am supposed to see," I screamed out in panic as I lowered my head in confusion. I noticed that I talked to the Hue only when I had discovered something new or when I was in an uncomfortable situation.

I was at the point where I felt like I had nothing left. I felt my mind go blank, the fight leave my body, and words go silent. I noticed for the first time while sitting in the Hue's energy that I felt exhausted. Why? Again my thoughts deepened, sinking into my past with the Hue and the visions of lessons learned. My mind continued to go deeper and allowed tension back into my body. With the self-awareness that crept back into my world, the Hue looked as if it was slowly regaining its magnificence. That's when I knew I had missed something. I again searched through the lessons, and as if it was an elephant in the room sitting right in front of me, I saw it.

Reaching to the sky, I pointed to the dark cloud and cried out, "The mist! I am missing the meaning of the mist."

The mist had been shadowing the brilliance of the Hue. Even though the Hue filled me with love and still flowed magnificently, the mist had been altering my view without me noticing. It had been there the entire time. The Hue, as if acknowledging my sudden awareness, had started to form the first background since my return. Regaining some confidence, I could see it was a different background than any that had come before. These were visions that seemed to flow in and out of each other. The mist was very visible in some, while in other backgrounds it didn't seem to exist at all. Different pockets of pictures flowed very quickly, too fast for me to gather any detail at all. It was like standing next to train tracks and trying to focus on a train car as it sped by right in front of me; by the time I had focused on a particular point, it was gone. I tried to change my position within the Hue to see if I could look longer at one picture, but nothing seemed to slow it down.

I took a deep breath, settled myself, and remembered to take it all in and see what was really in front of me. It was difficult not to add thoughts or speculation to what I was seeing. I reminded myself to live in the moment and observe what was given to me at the time. Really, the only thing I could make out was the mist. It was either present or nonexistent. The detail in the background, besides the mist, didn't seem to matter at that point.

I started to get used to the visions rushing around me, and I began to get the feeling again that I had missed something or that there was more for me to understand. As the thought crossed my mind, the Hue took it all away and brought back the calming flow of brilliant color while absorbing anxiety, which had started to build up in me again.

I knew there was more work, but with the speed that my world was flying around me, I felt there was no way I would be able to figure it out.

I was humbled by my inadequacies and yelled, "I know that a lesson is to be learned, but clearly I'm not Superman here!"

Within a millisecond, maybe even before I finished yelling, I was back on the path of life. It definitely was the same spot on the path that I'd visited the last time. It felt like a good place, yet I was surrounded by the darker tint of the mist, and an intense pain was radiating through my feet.

As I reflected back on my last visit, my perspective changed simultaneously as if my thoughts were still running behind the Hue's actions. This change of perspective took me above the path. The mist surrounded my body and certainly seemed to change my perspective of my position on the path. As I continued to ponder, I realized that the sheer lack of awareness or even accountability that got me to that spot on the path had to be similar to living life with blinders on. Had I been telling myself that life was so good that I was oblivious to the darkness surrounding me? "Have I become oblivious to the pain that I'm feeling and the pain I'm creating for others?"

My eyes dropped to the pathway in humility as my thoughts raced. I struggled with how I had become so insulated that I couldn't realize the pain surrounding me? I watched myself stand there uncomfortably and pondered what events had led me to convince myself that somehow I was content with my place in life. Had I lost touch with my emotions, my love for my wife, my children, and my job?

Looking out into the deep beauty of an unfocused future, I said, "Is that what I'm supposed to notice—the lack of perspective, the lack of awareness and accountability all rolled into one vision?" Before I finished, I knew that wasn't right. The Hue had continuously taken me deeper in these visions, and this would challenge me to search my understanding of myself to a new level.

The Hue removed me again as it absorbed the path of life. Before I could reflect on that experience, a background began to form. When it came into focus, the Hue had formed a very different background. It looked like church.

———

Growing up, I went to a private Lutheran school. Every Sunday, my parents would dress us three kids up in our Sunday best, and we would always sit in the same pew. As I learned about God and Jesus, I was taught that there was only one way to think about God. It was either right or wrong, a lesson later in life that seemed to be reasoned away.

This vision of the church had a collage of pictures that seemed to flow in a controlled order. There were clearly things or practices that I didn't recognize and others that I was very familiar with, such as the Bible, prayer, and communion. Regarding the other pieces of the vision, I wondered if I had really forgotten that much about my church experiences. I came to the conclusion that there were teachings that I didn't recognize. I wasn't sure if it was Jewish, Islamic, Buddhist, or something else, but they were clearly religious practices that I was unfamiliar with through my background in Christianity.

Even though I didn't have a knowledge base in all these areas, they all seemed to be from different religious ideologies. The energy felt like I was directed to look deeper, so I tried to focus on individual items. The more I zeroed in on particulars, the faster and more out of focus they became. It was as if looking deeper didn't mean looking harder at details.

When absent feelings rushed back into the Hue's show, I knew I had missed the lesson again. I centered myself to regain some perspective, and the lessons from the path of life swept through the vision as the collage of religion-based pictures continued to rotate by me. I remembered that my perspective was so misguided, I had convinced myself of a false reality. Then suddenly I realized that the mist was blanketing the entire vision of the church. It was like an awakening. I just wasn't sure of the meaning.

I noticed that even though the mist was part of the background, it didn't seem to have an impact on the surrounding Hue. An earlier vision, in which the mist had completely taken over the scene with its darkness and negative feelings—leaving me in panic—had no impact on the Hue working behind it. That became my biggest clue to the next lesson. No matter how overpowering the mist became, the Hue still functioned unaffected behind the scenes of every vision.

As I brought my hand to my chin to reflect, I asked, "How is this related to the path of life? How is this related to church?"

In the past, if I felt I had been losing ground on my lesson to be learned, it seemed that the Hue redirected me. "Or maybe I am searching in the wrong direction with a lack of perspective." I continued to piece the puzzle together. "If my perspective changes and I'm being self-aware, will that change the mist?"

I had become so entrenched in thought that I didn't realize that the Hue had changed the background right in front of me. I felt that, with a new piece of the puzzle I had seemingly stumbled upon, I was close to the answer. As I thought I was ready to finish this lesson, the background that formed looked to be another collage of times in my life.

Tracy and I were in all of them. There were kids in some and extended family in others, but the pattern was Tracy and I. Feeling that I needed to find the mist, I looked to the edges of the background and different scenes of the collage. I didn't pick up on any mist at all; in fact, all I felt was warmth, kindness, and love. I was still convinced the lesson had something to do with the mist. Then suddenly the Hue sent a burst of love through me. Like a shockwave, there was so much love flowing in the moments of the vision that I had become overwhelmed with emotion. Tracy and I were filled with an abundance of love and not shadowed by the darkness of the mist. Even though I was confused about the meaning, I knew it was important to solving this riddle.

I sat searching through the moments in my life surrounded by family, happiness, and love, and there was no mist to be found. The love we had for each other was quantified very early in our lives.

When I went from the Lutheran school to high school, we met in our freshman year. Girls weren't really my thing; they kind of scared me. Tracy wasn't exactly aggressive, but her friends knew she had a crush. They did all the dirty work for her, leaving messages and guiding her on flirtations. Tracy and I shared a lot of classes, but the one I remembered most was gym class. She was athletic and looked great in her gym shorts.

Tracy's interest peaked halfway through our freshman year. When she figured out I wasn't going to make a move, she had a friend set us up at a basketball game, and it was all over. It didn't take long for the two of us to realize the connection we had with each other. We spent most of our free time together and built an unusually strong foundation, even through our tumultuous teenage years. So young and inexperienced in life, we didn't realize our path would be traveled together, hand in hand. Only God knew the path we were about to travel.

As I collected myself, I realized the possibility that the mist was connected to me. I remembered feeling this way during my last visit to the Hue. I couldn't even begin to sift through all the past visions, but I needed to search for the conditions in which the mist existed inside the different scenes. I needed to know why it grew and turned to darkness.

As the stress of not knowing began to creep back into my mind, the Hue formed a familiar background. Sitting in front of me was the fast-paced collage of past visions. The mist was the key, evident in some areas and nonexistent in others. Purposely trying to see this vision from another perspective, I searched for a pattern. The mist had ties to emotional situations, false realities, personal ambitions, and maybe even a lack of empathy. With certainty, visions filled with emotions from an overactive mind supported the mist. As I looked deeper into those backgrounds with this broader perspective, everything slowed down as if I was on the right path to cracking the code. These pictures from my life were saturated with speculation, fear, and judgment. They weren't real. Did my mind create all of these in search of peace, power, or authority? I wasn't at that level yet and simply didn't know.

Finally, clenching my fist, I said, "They were created by my mind, hypothetical creations of my mind to take on the world in difficult situations! I was searching for control even if it was based on a false reality. My mind was trying to create a space for itself in a chaotic world."

As I quieted my voice back to thought, I realized that in most cases I was my own worst enemy. I had created moments of chaos to prepare for an event that would never happen, as if I wanted to be prepared for the worst-case scenario, or I would relive a moment to fix a feeling of inadequacy.

With a new awareness, the collage of Tracy and me reformed. The mist didn't seem to exist in this collage of happiness. Why were previous visions that included the two of us filled with the mist? Or were those mist-filled visions centered on me? Even though the creation of stressful hypothetical situations was a piece of the puzzle, it didn't totally fit.

As I was consumed by my past experiences in the Hue, energy began to take over with an undeniable feeling of love. Ignoring the awakening sign, I pondered deeper in thought. The battle for acceptance of love and hyperactive random thoughts intensified. However, the love-filled energy pushed out and overpowered all the mindless thoughts, leaving a sense of total peace. At that moment, I just existed—no battles in my mind, no judgments, just me, a small piece of all-existing energy.

"It's love, isn't it?" My emotion swelled, and I added, "No personal filtering or justifications, just love in its purest form."

Feeling that the mist had given up a huge piece of its existence, I started to explore the possibilities of the new findings and how free life could be without the haze of the mist hovering over every idea and thought. The mist couldn't exist in pure, judgment-free love.

The background shifted to what I would call world religions. The feeling of love slowly dissipated. Although love didn't disappear completely, it wasn't the focus of that vision. Feelings of superiority, hate, and arrogance swirled with compassion, forgiveness, love, and hope. How could religions, based on God, have negative connotations? Looking more like a fog draped over the individual illustrations, the mist was evident throughout. Its ghostly movements thinned in some areas where compassion lived and fogged in heavily with the negative emotions. It was difficult to separate the emotions tied to the competing views of God versus the emotions created by graciousness.

The world religions now appeared in cubes or boxes—tiny boxes that held meaning associated with each particular ideology. As I sat with the glory of the Hue in my presence, the vision continued to cycle and flow through the emotional backgrounds. It became clear that not only were the perspectives of different religions responsible for the negativity, but individual truth inside the religions had been overrun by human influence. My judgment-free thoughts continued to deepen to depths I had never experienced before in the Hue or in my life.

At times, togetherness filled the vision with solidarity and graciousness, and I felt the positive emotions lift my presence inside the Hue. Some views gave hope, forgiveness, and education about God, but I continued to feel an underlying sense of pain, fear, and dominance come through the mist. It was like everything great about God's true energy was shrouded by the ideologies of humanity. The mist seemed to represent the negative even when within the greatness of God.

"If God is the constant—if *you* are the constant, what is the variable? Is it the mist? Is it humankind?" My mind worked overtime, and my thoughts poured out of me as I continued to talk through it.

I sat in the presence of this vision, pondering God's existence. God is the constant in all religions. What is God? God is nature, people, the universe. God defines life's existence. God is everything. *God is energy!* As I raised my head from the depths of thought, I was unable to contain myself, so I yelled again, "God is energy! You are everything, every atom, every molecule known to man. You are the uninfluenced energy of the Hue!" My voice went silent as my thoughts tried to interject all the definitions that I had been taught way back in grade school.

So why was the mist flowing freely inside God? Why was there a negative side, a sense of humanity blanketing God? As if the lessons of newly acquired awareness rushed over me like a tsunami, I remembered that the Hue always operated independently of the mist. If the mist was as dark as the night sky, the Hue would still function in greatness beyond it.

As I raised my chin from my fist, my thoughts became words. "God, the mist isn't part of you; it's part of me. It's part of humanity! Human influences, including religion, are creations to give credence to the idea that humankind is the center of your creation—to give hope and definition to life itself. Religion defines people's vision of themselves." That moment of awareness could not be contained. My silent thoughts rambled as if a light to all secrets had been turned on.

My thoughts continued to flow quickly as if the final pieces of a puzzle were coming together. *Humans declare dominance over those who don't hold the same view of race, sex, and thought created by the arrogance of self-imposed greatness based on their ideology. These creations of differing views have become large enough to kill and start wars, yet you, God, continue to operate behind human ignorance in your full glory. Your greatness and simplicity is often overshadowed by our perspective and lack of awareness created by our own insecurities. Humans act as blind interpreters.*

The competing emotions in relation to good and bad became too exhausting. Even with the graciousness that humanity could give to the world, it drained my energy and left me feeling empty. I had finally let go.

Bowing my head in exhaustion, I tried to regain my composure. After what felt like only a few seconds, I looked up and saw that the Hue had never stopped working. It seemed that whenever I let go, the Hue filled me with a clear vision and truth—no interpretation needed.

Exhausted and not recognizing where the revelation came from, I said, "Man is the mist." Before I could repeat what I was sure was the answer to the riddle, the Hue swiftly took me back to the path of life. As the beauty of life formed around me, I declared again, "Man is the mist!"

I still stood in the middle of the jagged road, surrounded by beauty, love, and infinite dreams with the sweet smells of lilac and honeysuckle flowing in the soft breeze. I quickly came to realize that I hadn't hit the mark. The Hue changed the energy to redirect my attention. If the best of all things belonged to God's energy, how could the mist that manipulates accountability, self-awareness, and perspective exist in God's realm? It was beyond my comprehension, and I felt that blind faith in religion had made me unaware of the simple truth. The mist was the differentiation of one's self leading to a quest for power or a manipulation of one's reality. This was a self-created pain, a need for attention, and a confusion-based reality. This was a way to feel like I had control of my life.

I raised my hand back to my chin as I played with the riddle in my mind. "The mist isn't humanity; it's humanity's lack of perspective, self-awareness, and accountability. It is humanity identifying with all that differentiates itself from others." I rambled through my thoughts and stumbled across—*my ego*. Humbleness swept through the Hue as if my foolishness had been revealed to the world.

The mist faded into the horizon, leaving the path of life to reveal its true brilliance. My eyes and head slowly dropped as I peered through blooming flower gardens. Emotionally subdued, I said, "God, the mist is my ego, my own humanity. It is my search for control, attention, and differentiation."

In the awakening of that moment, a quote flowed through the Hue's energy. "Above all else, guard your heart, for everything you do flows from it" (Proverbs 4:23 NIV).

Not knowing the origin or who spoke those words, I reflected on what I felt. I found myself on the plushest part of the path of life in a surreal moment. The sights and smells were extravagant and greater than I had ever experienced, and there was no fear or analyzing, just love, peace, and most of all, hope. I had always felt I was knowledgeable about life, but I couldn't help but think about wisdom. *Does the ego take away wisdom? Does the ego detract from the ability to convey wisdom?* Either way, a calm mind separated from emotions allows greater vision.

"Bill, Bill, are you still with me here? We will be at the hospital in a few minutes! Are you comfortable? That morphine should be in full effect now." As the EMT adjusted my IV flow, I realized that I was back in my chaotic reality. I attempted a thumbs-up and murmured, "Good. Tracy?"

Leaning over me to take my vitals, the EMT said, "She's up front; she's here."

6

Certainty of the Unknown

*A*s the ambulance rolled up to the emergency-room doors, the gurney was met by a trauma crew and my in-laws, Robin and Flip. Tracy jumped out of the front seat and fell into her mother's arms. "It's bad. It's really bad, Mom!" she cried as they embraced. Nurses scurried around me, making sure I had IVs so I could be evaluated immediately by the doctor. As we waited, somewhat impatiently, Flip got a damp cloth and wiped away the evidence of the trauma from every part of my body, including my face, arms, and legs.

A defined visual that haunted my memory was when the doctor came in and spoke to Tracy. "There is nothing I can do to save his left arm. I can sew it up, but he'll never have function of it again." Robin, Tracy's mother, stepped in, saying, "Tracy, get him to U of M. Get him out of here now and to U of M." And with that, I was loaded back into the ambulance and on my way to the University of Michigan trauma unit.

I had become so unaware of what was happening around me that I didn't realize I had arrived at the new hospital. The morphine must have been in full swing. As I lay there in the trauma room, I had a tremendous pain in my lower back to the point that I couldn't lie in bed anymore.

The trauma doctor came in and had me walk him through the details of my accident, trying to gather information that might have led to a cause of my lower-back pain. "Mr. Lee, do you remember how you got down from the tree? Is it possible that you fell out of the tree?" As hard as I tried, the only visual of that moment was my son, Jacob, standing at the top of the hill.

The doctor grabbed a clipboard, made a notation, and handed it to the nurse. "Mr. Lee, we are going to take you up to x-ray. We have to eliminate the possibility that you fell out of the tree and fractured your back."

As all of the commotion continued, I focused on the conversation that the doctors were having with the man in the trauma bed next to me. I felt compassion for him as they talked about his injury. A high-pressure hydraulic line had impaled his leg and filled it with hydraulic fluid, stretching his skin like a balloon. As they talked about the possibilities of infection, I empathized and was relieved that it wasn't me over there in that bed. I wondered if he felt the same way I did when the doctor explained the injury to my arm. Was he happy that he wasn't me?

The nurses mobilized my bed by moving all my IV lines to the bed hook and rolled me away to x-ray. Minutes later, after the x-ray, the nurses rolled me back into the trauma room. They explained that my bladder was so full that it was backing up into my kidneys, creating the intense pain in my back. My body had become so tense from the shock that it wouldn't allow my urinary tract to function properly, so they had to catheterize me. No snapshot memory needed—that was not pleasant.

The trauma unit had gathered its finest hand surgeon and his team. I wouldn't find out until weeks later that he and his team of five specialty surgeons was one of the best in the world. As the team went through the lengthy and tedious procedure with Tracy, Robin, and Flip, I slipped away.

Due to the anesthetics, my perspective didn't move above as I went back into the Hue. Even though I was in good hands, I was overcome with gratitude for being back in the Hue. The places and feelings that I left behind were always filled with stress, fear, and negative emotions. Even though the Hue had put me through the paces, I always felt embraced by love.

As I settled in, the Hue's warm glow had a little extra squeeze on me. It felt like a bear hug, embracing me to the point where I knew I couldn't get away, yet it wasn't uncomfortable. I felt my emotions melt away as the energy blanketed me. I recognized that my mind had already started to think about the depth of this next lesson, but I couldn't help but wonder if the little extra warmth was in preparation for something difficult coming down the road. The Hue was always a step ahead of me. My anxiety was nearly gone when the first vision started to form. I wasn't sure at that point why I felt exhausted. I couldn't figure out if it was from being under anesthetics in my other reality or if letting go of my ego in the Hue left me with a lot of empty space to fill. The first vision had finished forming, and I felt emotionally drained.

Not wanting the Hue to take away its supportive energy, my shoulders slumped and my head followed. "Can you give me a minute here? I'm not sure that I have the energy to take this on right now."

Even in the midst of supportive love, I couldn't help but think of my future after the accident. My thoughts wandered from the Hue's background. Why was I so tired? Was I losing the battle in the operating room? Or was this—

My thoughts were abruptly interrupted by a vision that seemed to appear suddenly, as if to distract me. It was my wedding again. Tracy and I were standing on the platform in the front of the chapel, listening to the pastor as he read from the Bible. The room, like before, seemed dimly lit around everyone but Tracy and me. It looked like the chapel lights highlighted us. I couldn't tell if this was created from the mist or was actually lighting.

I looked deeper into the background, and I felt that the mist was created by all the doubt in the chapel that day. Yet Tracy and

I stood in the light of love—without doubt. As the perspective started to rotate in the room, I could see us from the front of the chapel. Again the darkness shadowed the onlookers. Even though I could feel both fear and excitement running through the Hue, I felt that my lesson was about Tracy and me. My thoughts began to ramble, trying to connect the dots with love, fear, and doubt. And then it was gone.

I continued to review my thoughts about what I had just seen. Tracy and I were not caught up in ego. We were not caught in the doubt that filled the room. We were back—in a collage. I found myself so entrenched in thought that I missed the collage of visions forming around me again. Thinking aloud as my eyes tried to focus on the newly formed background, I said, "How could I be so disconnected that I can't see the world forming right in front of me?" The collage was made up of Tracy and me working, raising our young children, date nights, and what seemed to be everyday events. However, one picture caught my eye. We were standing in a grocery store at the checkout. I could see numbers floating around. I felt anxiety and fear—or was it embarrassment? Tracy and I lived so tight from paycheck to paycheck that we had to add up our groceries as we shopped, fearing the embarrassment of having to remove items from the bag. The anxiety that took over the vision took me back to those days. The stress and anxiety had created arguments about the lack of money.

Another scene in the collage was one that I hadn't seen up to that point. My attention was directed to it—and it was about me. I was at my job again. I was very young and sitting in the office of my service manager, Ed. I could see that I was unhappy or—no, I was very upset and crying. Even though I've always worn my emotions on my sleeve, it wasn't like me to let go at work. Ed was trying to console me. What could bring that much emotion to my job that I couldn't contain myself?

As I started to feel myself being engulfed with the emotional scene, I remembered a day when I was a young man. Tracy had called me from her doctor's appointment. She tried to be brave over the phone, but her emotions spilled over with every word. She told me that they had found a lump in her breast.

I was totally invested in this scene of the collage. I found myself reliving that moment and feeling overcome with the fear of the unknown. A fear of losing the love of my life took control of the emotions running through the Hue. I was unfamiliar with breast cancer, and my mind filled in all the blanks with inaccuracies. Left up to its own devices, my mind created an overwhelming fear based on unknown facts. I had never worried about showing emotion in life, so why then? Was that important to my task in the Hue? With those questions, I was back in the Hue's embrace, surrounded by the warm, relaxing flow of spectacular color. It was like the Hue had squeezed the anxiety right out of me.

I couldn't help but let my mind go. I pushed my thoughts further than during previous visits and suddenly found myself back on the path of life. I was in the center of this vision. I had no real direction, and incredible signs of life surrounded me. Flowers bloomed, plush fields swelled with sweet fragrances rolling in a light breeze, and the horizon was filled with the grandest of snowcapped mountains sitting among strong, vibrant forests. I started to wonder if this was the way I should see my world, filled with nature, exploding with fragrance and color.

To keep myself from being swallowed up in the serenity, I quickly brought my focus back to the meaning. Why was I standing in the middle of this unbelievable view again? There didn't seem to be a path this time. I was just surrounded by greatness. Maybe my path was unwritten or maybe—

"Of course!" I yelled as I threw my hands up in the air. Then the Hue absorbed it and took it all away. "What in the world did I miss that time?" I asked halfheartedly. "I could use a little more time here to figure things out." I knew more would be coming.

I was back in the Hue's mystical flow only a moment before I found myself back at the altar. I recognized immediately the mist, the doubt, and the fear in the chapel. Knowing there was more, I searched for what had eluded me. The negative feelings began to dissipate as hope and confidence filled the space. These new emotions seemed to be coming from Tracy and me. I knew at the time that I absolutely wanted to marry this girl, even though we still had a full year of high school to complete. I knew that I loved her and Ashley more than anything I had ever known at such a young age. I had no idea how it would work. I just knew. I just knew—

That was my clue. Quickly the Hue brought me back to the collage. I saw our day at the Jackson Fair, shortly after we'd found out we were going to have a baby. I saw the grocery store checkout filled with anxiety and the fear brought on by Tracy's doctor visit. What did I *know* about these snippets of my life?

There were so many emotions connected to these memories that confusion began to fill my head. Having learned from my previous lessons in the Hue, I figuratively stepped back from my thoughts and just took it all in. I knew there would be a common thread, and I tried to contain my impatience. All I could see was frustration, fear, anxiety, and—"Wait!" As I redirected my thoughts, I said, "I am seeing all the negative emotions again!" Bringing the palms of my hands to my temples, I tried to focus and clear my thoughts. I was acknowledging the emotions, and I was aware of everything happening in those moments. There didn't seem to be any complications or interference from the mist. "So what am I missing?"

The collage seemed to center itself again, focusing my attention on a new picture from my past. I was back in grade school. Some of my favorite teachers came into view. They were teaching lessons about life. Some lessons were from the Bible, from athletic activities, and from friendships in class. Again confusion started to cloud my mind. I suddenly found myself overthinking and bringing on a self-imposed pressure to solve the puzzle. I was unaware of how much pressure I had created until the Hue pulled the vision away. I found myself settling in the flow of color and energy, returning to my calmness.

I centered myself and brought my hands to a position of prayer. "Lord, it seems no matter what lessons I've learned, I default back into a position of panic. I step back to a comfortable place filled with fear and anxiety, where my mind runs wild. I have such a lack of—"

Maybe because I was getting ahead of myself, the Hue took me back to the path of life. I lost my train of thought as the magnificence of life quickly formed around me. Having no idea what I had been about to say, I found myself in awe of life's offering. It had been so easy to take refuge on the path of life and just dream, just let everything go, and imagine whatever future I could create. I started to reflect on what the Hue had shown me during that visit and wondered if I had somehow limited myself again to small dreams. Had I allowed the *how* of a dream to crush the dream itself? Had I disappointed Tracy or myself? What about my kids? Did I not dream big enough to fill their lives?

I felt the perspective in the Hue changing. The path of life was rotating or directing my focus to a specific area. I could see what looked like several paths, each winding in different directions, but all coming together in the distant. Some paths led through darkness and rough terrain, while others had a more consistent path. No matter what, each path had varying levels of terrain. Some had much darkness while others winded through a visibly brighter terrain. No path was without a rough patch or dim spot. It was the balance of each that differed greatly between paths.

"Is that fate?" I brought my hand to my chin as I gathered my thoughts. "No matter what path I take—the jagged road filled with sharp stones or the path leading into the darkness of the forest or the path through fields of beautiful flowers—I will eventually end up at a fixed point. Is that fixed point death?" My thoughts were firing off like popcorn in a popcorn maker. Then everything stopped suddenly.

It was as if the Hue had grabbed my mind and frozen all my thoughts. The quick-fire random thoughts didn't help my centering. I felt like I was going in the right direction, but maybe my mind had again gotten in the way of truth.

The Hue had taken me back to a revolving collage of the vision—with one major difference. All the emotions that had been so overwhelming were not present. I felt confident that everything was going to be okay. I began to believe that human reality is just an ignorance of life itself. When I saw all these moments with no emotions attached, my sense of awareness changed. It was like watching a scary movie with the sound turned off. The emotional reaction to sound was gone. Just the truth remained.

I couldn't help but go back to thinking about the path of life. All paths ended up in the same spot. Some paths are shorter and more treacherous while others have a grand view of life. The intersection of these paths was critical to this lesson. Whether the intersection was fate or death, the solution to all these visions was related to my attitude about life, even if I couldn't see the effects.

I knew the people in my life at different times were there to teach me. Teaching came in two different forms: things I needed to emulate to be successful and lessons to be learned by not repeating a particular behavior. What I knew was that God had taken care of Tracy and me through everything, just like we believed we—

Hue quickly took me back to the path of life, and I felt I knew the answer to the riddle. With a fist pump in the air, I yelled, "It's faith!" I repeated the fist pump and said in an exuberant voice, "It is faith! All of our trials and tribulations in life are overcome by faith. Remove the noise in everyday life—doubt, fear, and anxiety—and take action through faith to accomplish anything."

As I finished yelling into the serene setting, another quotation filled the energy as if God himself were speaking to me. The energy carried this quote with passion as it filled my spirit: "Now faith is confidence in what we hope for and assurance about what we do not see" (Hebrews 11:1 NIV). Over and over again, the energy carried this message, and it became clear that Tracy and I always knew what was true to our hearts, and our actions followed. Faith is just a dream without action. Love and faith shielded Tracy and me from the doubt of others, no matter what path we stood on. Faith with action was my answer.

I found myself struggling to keep my eyes open in an unfamiliar environment as my return to the harsh reality was much calmer this time. My mind, however, was in a peaceful place as the lessons of the Hue settled deep into my conscience.

7

A Miracle of Healing

"Mr. Lee, how are you?" Groggy and unaware of where I was, I heard an unfamiliar voice coming from the end of my bed. As I looked over to the side of the bed and slowly gained focus, I could see two men dressed in white coats. "Mr. Lee, I'm sure you don't remember me from last night, but I am Dr. Lou. My team and I, for about four hours, put your arm back together last night. It took five surgeons, including our neurosurgeon, to get everything back together as well as we could."

The doctor raised his left arm and referenced from his wrist to about four inches up his forearm, he continued. "Imagine everything from here to here being removed with at least a quarter inch of material missing." He then gestured with his right hand, showing me where the damage was done. "Your ulnar nerve and artery were destroyed. I performed a loop tie around the mesh point of the nerve for a future reference point, where eventually I will have to go back in and perform a nerve graft. The ulnar artery I simply sewed shut.

"Your body will grow new veins to supply your hand, and you still have your radial artery to supply blood flow. Your hand is in that folded-down position"—he demonstrated a clawed

hand—"because we had to put all of your tendons back together."
As his intern stepped around the side of my bed, Dr. Lou continued.
"That cast on your arm goes all the way up to your shoulder to
prevent all possible movement in your hand and arm. Your arm is
in an absorbent cast until at least next week. Because of the extent
of damage and the open wound, we are going to send you home
today. You stand a much better chance of not getting an infection
at home than here in the hospital, since your immune system is
used to the environment at your house. A staph infection would
be devastating this early in the healing process."

I knew I was hearing Dr. Lou, but I wasn't grasping everything
he said. My head was so cloudy I couldn't focus. "So, when am I
going home?"

"The nurses will get your dismissal paperwork together and
go over it with your wife." As he stepped closer to me and rested
his hand on my right arm, the tone in his voice deepened. "This
is still a very serious injury. Our first order is to keep an infection
from happening. Our second order is to save the arm, and the
third order is help you regain as much mobility as possible. This
is going to be a very long process, and you will need full-time help
at home for a minimum of one to two months."

As my eyes welled up, I nodded. "I understand."

"Okay then, do you have any other questions? If not, I will see
you in a week, and we will get that cast off to look for any signs
of infection."

"Doc, one question," I said as I tried to scoot my way back in
the bed to sit up. "How many stitches?"

With a smirk, as if he knew I was asking for a badge of honor,
he said, "Too many to count." And they disappeared around the
corner.

I wasn't sure how many hours had passed, but my next visitor
was a welcome face. As I slowly came to again, Tracy reached
over and clutched my hand, asking in an emotional tone, "Are
you okay?"

The comfort of her voice stroked my emotions like a soft touch through my hair as my eyes began to well with comforting tears. I rolled my head over on the pillow because it felt too heavy to lift. In a quivering, soft voice, I asked, "Are *you* okay?" As I felt her emotional energy through a squeeze of my hand, she nodded slightly. "When do we go home?"

She stood from her chair, holding my right hand firmly. I could see a look of relief through the terror still in her weary eyes. My accident had taken a heavy toll on her. "We'll be checking out soon."

Not long after, the head nurse walked in and asked, "Are we ready to get out of here?" Overcome by exhaustion, we both nodded. The nurse went on to explain that I was on a triplicate narcotic, because the wound under the cast was open, so the nerve and tendons were exposed. "This narcotic will help take the edge off. You will need help doing everything—and I mean everything. You'll most likely experience hallucinations and some wild dreams while on this medication. Next week, we will see you back here for evaluation. We will cut off the cast and then most likely put another one on that will be removable so someone can bandage your arm two to three times a day." She moved to my bedside. "But first things first. Let's get this IV and catheter out. I have a wheelchair ordered up, and I would suggest that you have a wheelchair delivered to your home. This will allow you to get outside eventually and move around your house easier."

As I slowly got out of bed and into the recently delivered wheelchair, weary random thoughts provoked by fear began to enter my head. *How long is this process going to take? Will we be able to pay for it?* The fogginess from the narcotic gave me little recollection of what had transpired with the Hue, as if it had all been a dream. It was similar to the moment when you wake up and you're aware that you had a dream, but you have a difficult time remembering details.

My memories of the next week are an emotional blur. My days

were filled with sorrow, fear, and plenty of tears while my nights were engulfed in sweat-filled nightmares. Several friends stopped by the house, and my parents came home from Florida a few days after the accident. As my father came to my side, I couldn't hold my emotions. "Dad, I really screwed up this time." I didn't recall any response, just that it seemed somehow I had let him down.

It was time. The first week had come to an end, and we headed back to the University of Michigan for my first follow-up. Tracy made sure to follow their instructions and gave me a full dose of pain medication before we left. With an undeniable stench coming from the cast, we started our forty-five-minute drive. My nerves were starting to kick in, and I looked over at Tracy as she focused on the road. "You know this will be the first time."

She glanced over and took her right hand off the wheel to touch my arm. "The first time for what, honey?"

My eyes began to fill again with an abundance of tears, something that happened often. "My first time to see my arm; I still haven't seen my arm." With a little squeeze from her hand, silence settled in for the rest of the ride.

As we rolled up to the Taubman Center at the University of Michigan, my mother, who had driven down from Okemos to join us, was there waiting at the entrance. As we made our way back through the halls, we were greeted and asked to come back to an exam room.

Not seeing my doctor, I asked, "Is Dr. Lou going to be here?"

The assistant glanced over his shoulder. "We will get the cast off and ready for inspection, and he will come in to evaluate it. By the way, did you take your pain medication?"

Tracy stepped around, holding my right arm as if to steady me. "Yes, about an hour ago."

The medical assistant pivoted as he pointed to a door. "That's good. Step on in, and we'll get started."

I sat with my arm elevated in a type of lounge chair, and he began to cut the cast off. My mother and Tracy sat next to me, watching intently. As he finished making the cut, he looked me straight in my eye. "Are you ready for this?" Not knowing what to expect, I simply nodded. I could feel the tension building from my shoulders down. He removed the upper section from my fingertips to my shoulder. "Make sure you do not try to move or straighten your arm or fingers."

It became evident right away that I wasn't going to be moving anything. As the top of the cast came off, there was an incredible pain and an intense stench of death. The pain was so intense, I couldn't pinpoint an origin. It was like my entire arm was on fire.

"Now for the tough part," he said as he grabbed my arm and rotated it to remove the lower part of the cast. The pain intensified to the point that my mother started to fire off random questions to try to divert my attention.

The medical assistant said as our eyes met again, "Mr. Lee, I need to remove all these bandages now and clean the wound." I felt myself settle into a toughness mindset, just as I had during my football days.

I asked as he continued to unwrap, "What is that smell?" As the final few pieces came off my arm, I could see the answer that he was about to give me.

"Mr. Lee, the doctor will be in soon to go over everything with you. The smell is the flesh and soft tissue that no longer has blood supply."

I couldn't believe what I was looking at. My mother abruptly stood up and left the room. Tracy and I just stared at it as she held my right hand; our muscles were synchronized in tension. My eyes began to well up again as I looked at the atrocity that was my left arm. As it lay there lifeless on the armrest, I just couldn't come to grips with what I was looking at. There was a gaping hole in my arm. A large piece was simply missing; there was no skin or flesh—just tendons that looked like small white straws. My arm was missing so much soft tissue that I couldn't wrap my head around how in the world it would ever heal. As I continued to inspect the trauma in awe, the doctor walked into the exam room. I was speechless.

In an upbeat voice, the doctor said, "Well, how's it looking? Is this the first time you've seen it?"

I was still stunned. "My arm doesn't look fixed. There's a huge hole. I can see things I'm not supposed to be able to see."

"Well, let's take a look here." He pulled up a stool and gently started to wipe my arm with a clean cloth. "Mr. Lee," he said as he started dabbing dried blood from the wound, "you had an extreme trauma to your arm and hand. We were able to stitch up your hand, but your arm we had to rebuild. There was nothing to stitch up on the outside. Trust me, the human body is incredible, and that four-inch hole will eventually close."

As he rotated my arm back toward him, the pain was so intense, it shot up into my shoulder. Pointing to specific parts of the trauma, he said, "These tendons were all severed. That's why you had no function in your hand. The ulnar nerve right down here"—he continued to clean—"was so badly torn apart, I simply took the two shredded ends, matched them up, and did a loop tie around it for a future reference point. We will have to do a nerve graft to help get some function and feeling back in your hand." He went on to explain the function of the ulnar nerve and ulnar artery. I was so mesmerized by that hole in my arm, I just zoned out.

He started to explain the critical nature of the next few weeks. "We have to get things right here. Infections, especially a staph infection, could result in you losing your arm. If the smell gets any worse, I need you to come in here immediately. These antibiotics will help, but you need to be aware that these next few weeks are critical."

As if I didn't understand, I asked the presumptive question. "How could the smell get any worse?" Continuing with a bit of positivity, I added, "How long will it be before I can lift weights again?"

With just a smile, he said, "Right now, let's get this hole in your arm closed up. I'm not sure you'll ever be able to lift weights with this arm again." Stunned by what I heard, I glanced over at Tracy as a tear ran down my cheek. The doctor added, "Let's get a two-piece cast on you here and get you some care instructions."

As he stood up and grabbed a bundle of bandages and wraps, he said, "I will see you once a week to monitor this. And trust me, if you take care of this, the hole will form scar tissue and heal up." He sat back down and gently picked up my arm. "It was weightlifting that helped save your arm, and with your body in great shape, it will heal quicker. We generally see athlete's bodies heal faster and better. The size of your arm and muscle structure helped save it. Most people with this type of trauma lose their arm completely."

Tracy squeezed my right arm, as if to reassure me, and said, "See, all that work at the gym paid off."

As soon as the doctor left, the assistant started to fit me with a new the cast. "Well, what color of cast do you want?"

Glancing over the assistant's shoulder, I asked, "What colors do you have?" He reached around to the counter and showed me an array of colorful materials. Right away I knew. "Green!" I was sitting in the trauma center of the University of Michigan, but I couldn't let go of my Spartan green.

After a few minutes, we were on our way. As we met back up with my mother in the hallway, my arm finally started to relax, and the pain subsided. As Tracy held me tight, my mother muttered, "I just couldn't watch any longer, seeing my son in so much pain." With a squeeze of my hand, she added, "I'm sorry. I just had to leave."

Within minutes, we found ourselves back at our cars and on our way home. Back at home, Tracy and I reflected on the visit. She could see that I wasn't handling the news very well. "No matter what, Bill, we will survive."

I laid down on the couch slowly to gather my thoughts. I

looked up at Tracy. "How are we going to pay our bills? How are we—"

She laid her hand on the top my head. "We have made it through all our challenges in life. We will make it through this. I don't care if we have to sell our house. We will survive, because we have each other. Nothing outside our family matters. All of this"—she pointed around the room—"can be replaced. My husband and the father of our children cannot."

The next three weeks were full of doctor visits and rest. My mind was pretty disabled by the narcotics. The dreams at night were horrifying. There were no visits into the Hue. In fact, the distant memory of my visits and the Hue itself were quizzical at best, a vague recollection that had faded into oblivion. My pastor made some house calls, and volunteers from the church continued to bring dinners to our home.

As the weeks continued, a deep, unexplainable feeling started to take over my thoughts. These thoughts were soulful and spiritual—as if my experience in the Hue was returning, and my mind had opened up to a whole new perspective of my world. I was open to the unexplainable and had an insight that felt mystically strange: I could see people's true selves, especially when they weren't being genuine. I would bury this insight for months to come.

My fourth weekly visit came up fast. The last few visits had been pretty routine; however, this visit would throw a twist into the mix. Dr. Lou came into the room and greeted us. "How is the arm doing today?"

I nodded. "I can see a difference in the size of the hole."

He walked over to the exam table. "That's good. We're a long way from getting this thing into therapy though. It has been thirty days since we put you on this narcotic. We're taking you off of it today." He picked up his clipboard and began to write a new prescription. "That medication is extremely addictive, and we have to move you off of it right now, before we have problems."

"Okay, Doc. I feel a strange sensation in the lower palm of my hand and sometimes up in my fingers."

He removed the temporary cast and examined my hand. "The old nerve is dying off. So you're getting a sensation in the hand that isn't real." He again explained the reality of my damaged hand and how a nerve graft would be necessary.

I struggled severely from withdrawals of the narcotic over the next couple of weeks. I felt like I couldn't control myself, and I had nervous ticks. Within a few weeks later, those subsided. Even though I still woke up regularly throughout the night in a panic, the nightmares weren't as intense.

Week ten was an exceptional visit. The doctor had about ten interns following him around that day, and as usual, he walked into the room and asked, "How's that arm today? Let's take a look at it." As he removed my temporary cast, he was pleasantly surprised to see that the hole in my arm was nearly closed. "Boy, we are making some progress here, aren't we?"

I sat up with a little boost of energy. "Yes, I can't believe it actually closed." I fumbled for my next words, because I could feel something special going on, but I didn't know how to explain it to him. "Doc, that feeling in my hand is getting more intense. It feels like—like it is growing."

As he got ready to leave the room, he said, "Well, it can take weeks for that nerve to die off. We'll schedule some therapy in a week. That hole should be completely closed by then."

As the assistant came in to dress my arm, I felt my hopes had been dashed; he had completely dismissed what I told him. I knew my body, and what was happening in my hand was not death. It was life.

The next couple of weeks flew by, and it was time to start therapy. It would be the first time my hand would move in more than twelve weeks. The cast was gone, and I could see the impact of having no movement from my hand. The "belly" of my forearm was gone; wrist to elbow was all bone. My hand looked like it had died. It was nearly all bone too.

The woman therapist proved to me that there was much worse that I couldn't see. After the routine storytelling, she took my hand and straightened each finger and then worked each individual knuckle. The pain was very intense—bone on bone. It was like trying to get a rusty nut and bolt apart that had been fused together by time. There was no lube in the joints. Besides the accident, this was easily the most painful thing I had ever experienced. After she so-called "loosened up" my hand, it was time for a couple of tests.

The therapist handed me a grip tool to measure my hand's grip strength. My right hand's strength was off the chart. But my left hand measured about one and half pounds of grip strength. I was in shock, and I felt the onslaught of emotions. This first measurable result showed how much work was to come.

The next test was a sensitivity test. Before she started, I told her that I had a strange feeling that continued to grow in the base of my palm. I told her that the doctor had said the old nerve was dying off, but I felt differently. I couldn't explain it to her or the doctor; I just knew something was happening.

As she picked up the little tools with different sized bristles to test sensitivity, she said, "We will see right now." When she performed the test and wrote the results down on a drawing of a hand, I could see that I had feeling in my wrist and lower palm.

With a burst of excitement, I said, "It's there, isn't it? I have feeling in my hand!"

She continued to finish the test, she answered, "We will let the doctor review the results."

No matter what, I had a newfound confidence given to me through what I was sure was a miracle.

After the first visit, the therapist gave me specific exercises for homework. My disciplines from football kicked in again. I needed complete focus to push through the pain and not quit. Day in and day out, I worked each knuckle over and over again. Three days a week, the therapist worked me over, and it didn't take long to see and feel results.

After a few weeks—and not waiting for a release from the doctor—I knew my body was ready to start lifting weights again. I grabbed a five-pound dumbbell in my left hand. The cold steel against a still dilapidated, boney hand was a stark reminder of the road ahead. My left hand had lost so much soft tissue, it created a whole new challenge. Just gripping a dumbbell caused intense pain. I pressed forward for another week, and soon it was time for my first doctor's review since the nerve sensitivity test.

I drove myself there for the first time, and as I arrived, I felt an incredible positive energy. As I went back into the exam room, I saw Dr. Lou surrounded by several interns. After a few minutes, he came into the room. "How's that arm today?" I told him it felt great, not telling him that I had started lifting weights again.

He grabbed my file and asked, "Have you started therapy yet?"

"I have, and I also had the nerve sensitivity test," I said with excitement in my voice. He looked through the papers and glanced up over his glasses at me. Then he turned around and walked out of the room. A little confused by his exit, I heard him in the hallway, talking to another doctor. "You need to come take a look at this. I can't believe this. Come in here right now and read this report."

As he and two other doctors entered the room, I could see the befuddled look on Dr. Lou's face. The other two doctors read my charts, flipping through pages. They looked up at me simultaneously. One of them said, "You have feeling in your hand?"

Beaming with confidence, I said, "I do. I have said it for weeks, and nobody believed me."

One of the doctors cradled my arm. "You can feel this?"

Smiling from ear to ear, I said, "Yes sir, it's tingly, but I can feel the corner of my palm."

Dr. Lou came over to my bedside and continued the examination of my hand. "There was so much damage that I just shoved the two frayed ends together and did a loop tie for a reference point. I must have done a better job than I thought. Nerves don't just regenerate. We will watch this situation, but if this continues, we will not want to mess around with a nerve graft. We could do more damage than good."

As he finished, I knew this was at least the second miracle in the last several weeks that I had experienced. It was a great moment, having come out of this tragedy. Little did I know this was just the beginning of amazing things to come. But first there would be more personal pain that would challenge Tracy and me. Those times would challenge our commitment and our support of each other.

8

Transcendent Path

*I*t was November, four months after my accident, and time for my last visit to the U of M. Tracy and I traveled together for this momentous occasion. My nerve had regenerated, and I had gained an incredible amount of muscle back in that short time. I'd had an additional minor surgery a few weeks earlier to free scar tissue that was binding my tendons and reducing my movement.

When Tracy and I walked in and sat down, we couldn't help but notice some new patients sitting in the waiting room. It was clear that their journeys were just beginning. At the same time, we reached for each other's hands in recognition of the journey we had traveled up to that point.

We were shown the way back to the exam room, a path well traveled by the two of us. As we waited for Dr. Lou to come in the room, I looked at Tracy. "I can't believe it's over."

She leaned over, rubbing my arm. "Thank God for everything we've gone through and that we came out together."

Dr. Lou came in and went over my final visit, making sure I had no concerns. The visit was short and sweet. When we exited, we made sure to say goodbye to all the nurses and assistants that had been so gracious to us over the past several months. We went down to the therapy room and dropped off a baby gift for the therapist that had forced me to go through some of the most painful exercises I had ever done. It had been clear that the barrier of pain was mine to surrender to or move through, as if it was my first test from God. How hard was I willing to work to regain the use of my arm? Her persistence was one of the greatest gifts I received.

As we left the hospital, even though I had great joy that it was over, I had heartache because I was leaving a number of people behind that had become like family.

Tracy and I had been back to work full time for a couple of months, and we had kept up with our bills with the help of family. When I returned to work, my job was indescribably different. There was something very different about my sense of self in the company, as if the fight had been taken out of me. At least I was less engaged in the competitive world. I'm not sure, but it was as if my ego had been wiped clean, like the mist had been cleared. I could have chosen to ignore this new journey, but I chose to travel.

I wasn't sure if the visits in the Hue had created this new me, but I couldn't keep my mind from dreaming. I had an insatiable need for knowledge. I bought books about logic, ego, and philosophy. I made a call to Spring Arbor College about finishing my degree. Though I didn't go back to school at that time, that phone call would become a defining moment.

A few months went by, and I started to engage in some old behaviors. Another department manager and I had a conflict that was really the fault of the system we worked in at the shop. I frequented my memory of the Hue and recalled key lessons to try and minimize the mist shadowing my life. We just couldn't help but have conflicts, and I still hadn't developed the disciplines instilled by the Hue.

With the one-year anniversary of my accident approaching, another life-changing event was about to take place. My boss made an unannounced visit to the location I was managing. As we drove to lunch, I could feel an unusual amount of tension in the car. Five minutes into lunch, he said that I didn't appear to be happy at my job. He also told me that my attitude was creating tension among the other managers. As I listened, I couldn't help but think he was talking about himself. Then he fired me. There I was, sitting at lunch with a meal on the way, and I was jobless. My boss continued on in normal conversation as if my life had not been altered. In that moment, I lost all ability to see any of the Hue's lessons. I was so upset, I couldn't get out of there quick enough. I was very confused about what had just happened.

As soon as we got back to the office, my boss watched me pack my things and questioned everything that I took as if I wanted to steal trade secrets. I was nothing more than an ex-employee, as if I had stolen from him in the past. I knew my boss, and though I didn't view life the same way, that was over the top. I had felt an unusual tension since I returned to work. I had gotten the impression I wasn't good enough because I had lost my competitive edge. But somewhere down the line, I had let the darkness of the mist take over my life again.

I called Tracy and told her what happened. She left her job early in Lansing as I sat at home, still holding onto the confused anger in my heart. If the mist had ever been present in my life, it was then. Everything was dark. Everything was filled with anger, pain, loneliness, and fear. I felt that all the years I was underpaid and worked sixty to eighty hours a week on salary had been completely dismissed. The ego that had virtually disappeared months before was back with a vengeance. It was as if it had been looking for an opening to take back control, and it found it.

After the shock had settled, Tracy and I had to scramble. Amazingly, I could feel my heart soften. It was as if I had lived in a partly cloudy day. When a cloud would block the light from the sun, the mist would bring in fear and anger rather than the sun illuminating all the possibilities life could bring. When I had direction, Tracy and I had peace and faith.

Tracy had found herself in a similar position months earlier as she made extra efforts to comfort me. It seemed routine for her to hold me. "We have made it through worse things, and we will prevail," she said. I wasn't sure where her strength came from, because she didn't have an easy upbringing. She again was my foundation.

For the first time, I went down to the unemployment office. After I started receiving my unemployment checks, I put a plan together to start my own business. A month later, I began a business in the automotive industry doing mobile oil changes. I called it One Man and an Oil Can. I began calling on local businesses, and it struck a chord right away with small-fleet owners.

Tracy and I were still in a lot of debt and behind in paying bills. The business showed promise, and it was growing slowly. We looked at the possibility of filing for bankruptcy, but Tracy and I knew that wasn't the right thing to do. So we stuck it out. I knew I had to grind it out hard for the business to be successful. In the midst of all the hurry, I hadn't taken time to relate our experiences to the lessons of the Hue. I hadn't taken time to reflect at all.

The first anniversary of my accident was coming around, and Tracy and I decided it would be celebrated like a birthday from then on out. We went to the store to buy a cake. We were talking about what we could call this special day, and I said, "We should call this day a Celebration of Life day. We need to remember the day when all life came to a halt—a reset, so to speak—a change in our lives forever."

Tracy picked out a cake and said, "I like it. We'll celebrate this day with our anniversary every year."

Tracy and I had no idea what was still to come. In fact, it would take another two years before the distant horizon on the path of life would start to come into focus. We relied on prayer, hard work, and her family. My attention was so focused on fixing the problem that I lost my peripheral vision, including not paying much attention to the kids. As life seemed to be coming around, I felt swallowed up by it. My life was returning to an old recognizable chaos, an unobserved way of life.

Soon the business started paying the bills and making a little money, but I knew it wasn't my future. As well as it was doing, my heart wasn't in it. The lessons of the Hue continued to work inside me, and I could feel something bigger for my life. I just had no idea what it meant or where to look.

It had been several months since I'd seen or talked with my old boss when he left a message seemingly out of the blue. With curiosity, I called him back. I found it strange yet enticing to hear his voice. I still had some anger, but it was overshadowed by all the good years we'd worked together. I could hear an unusual nervousness behind his typical matter-of-fact voice. Then he said, "I would like to talk to you about coming back to work for me. I would like to sit down with you and Tracy to see if there's a plan that we can make work for all of us."

I was cautiously optimistic, and I didn't have the time to hold on to the negative feelings from the past. I believe the lessons from the Hue had intervened in my growth, providing me with focus to overcome the mist. I took accountability for my part, whether I thought it was fair or not. I acknowledged the fear and anger, and I moved on, leaving my ego—the darkness of the mist—behind.

Nervous myself, I called him back. I glanced over at Tracy, who was sitting in the kitchen. And I said, "I can talk to Tracy and see if we can make a specific date work."

With what sounded like a sigh of relief, he said, "I would really appreciate that. By the way, I received a phone call for Bill from some college about night classes. They left a name and number stating that they have a new class beginning in January. I assume this message was for you." As he gave me the name and number, I barely remembered that I had called them a year earlier.

I couldn't help but wonder, *Why now?* It felt like a push in a specific direction, like a calling that stood out to me or a calling that may have been missed before the visit in the Hue. A conversation with my old boss had opened up a new path, just like the vision on the path of life. That phone call was meant to be a defining moment, and I had to be in a mist-free place to be able to see it.

I called the local college and set up an appointment to look into the program, and it didn't take long for me to say yes. I felt an incredible presence, as if I had been chosen to be in that class. I knew that I would have to borrow money to finish my education, but I also was aware that I wasn't happy with my career. There was no post-accident confusion that success and happiness don't always go together. I had taken something that I had knowledge in and created a business, but I wasn't happy with that direction.

As the day came for our meeting, my old boss invited Tracy and me to their Christmas gathering with the other managers, which felt a little odd. Tracy and I had almost filed for bankruptcy after I got fired, and now we were sitting in front of the man who had fired me. But I wouldn't have been on that new path if I hadn't been fired. I wouldn't have been enrolled in college to finish my education. I would have slowly fallen back into my old routine, and again life would have been running me instead of me living it. The Hue's perspective was at work again. Tracy always had a calm demeanor, and she helped me keep it together that day. Yet the mist was constantly trying to push its way into my thoughts.

As we sat down in a private office, my boss said, "Well, I have a management position for our parts department open. Is that something you would be interested in?"

I found it intriguing, and my thoughts went back to all the decisions I'd made when a carrot had been hung out before me. As if I had returned to the Hue, I saw past decisions based on an easier route that led to unhappiness. "I will talk to Tracy about it and let you know next week. I've enrolled in evening classes at Spring Arbor College to finish my degree. They're on Thursday nights, so I would have to leave work early on Thursdays."

As we stood up to go join the others in the living room, he shook my hand and said, "Okay, I'm sure we can make that work. We will talk more about it after you talk with Tracy."

Christmas had passed, and Tracy and I talked about the possibility of me quitting my growing business and returning to my old employer. "You know nothing has changed since you were fired," she said. "The situation will be the same old headaches."

I lowered my head in thought, then said, "I know, dear, but I'm enrolled in college again, and that will lead to a better future. If he agrees to me leaving early on Thursdays, I think—for the big picture—this will help take the financial pressure off. I'm doing this for our end goal, not his."

She reached out to me. "I will support whatever decision you make."

That evening, I decided to sell my business equipment and take the job. I knew it would be the best way for me to earn a living and finish my education at the same time. Whatever humility would be involved in returning to the shop, I knew the big picture was now my big picture.

A couple of weeks later, my first class started, and a dynamic teacher named Eve would be teaching most of our classes on Thursday nights. When she walked into class, she brought a calm, caring heart with her. She had a loving attitude that the class of twenty or so seemed to latch on to. Our class was made up of similar individuals with college experience looking for a new path in life. I didn't know it at that time, but Eve was the professor I needed at that time in my life. She was the next piece of the puzzle. She talked a lot about clarity and centering the spirit. My life was out of touch with religion, but with God I had entered a deeper spiritual place that I didn't know how to explain to people, including Tracy. I felt that Eve was going to be able to help me develop that inner spirit, and I would not be disappointed.

Every weekend that went by, Tracy and I talked about the separation between religion and God. It seemed clear to me, as if the Hue had wiped out the mist in everything, including the ideology of religion. I recalled the lessons that the Hue had presented in the collage of scenes from church and religions around the world. I could feel things as genuine or disingenuous as they actually were in life. Because of my inability to verbalize this, it felt more like a curse than a gift. People were unwilling to let go of what they had been taught throughout life, even if the ideological belief was clearly connected to ego and had nothing to do with God. I continued to read and write as if an artesian well of feelings couldn't be shut off.

As I gained a more trusting relationship with others in my class, I opened up, sharing deep feelings and the details of my accident. The more I shared, the more it flowed out of me. It actually seemed to be therapeutic for others in the class as well. The big guy in class letting go and talking about emotional things gave them an opening to do the same.

Although my job was going well, the business wasn't in good shape. In the fall of 2000, I was halfway done with my degree, and my boss was searching for a buyer. I had another six months before my degree would be finished, and another long-term manager had already decided to leave the company. A buyer had been found, and it felt refreshing when I met with the new owners. Although their ways were different, we blended well.

A couple of months had gone by, and everything seemed to be going okay with the new ownership—until the day came when they discovered a discrepancy in the books, a mistake that had been made when the deal was written. A buzz was going around the shop like wildfire, but I didn't feel nervous. Maybe that's because I had already been through being fired a year and a half earlier.

Next thing I knew, the old owner was packing his office. He was experiencing the same emotions that I had gone through. An honest mistake or oversight allowed me to watch my old boss go through what he had put me through. It was a strange twist of fate, for sure.

The Hue had taught me humility, so nowhere in my heart did I have room for a "what goes around comes around attitude." He was angry, bitter, and promised legal action. I felt calm, as if the Hue had taught me that life does go on. I knew my old boss would have to let go of that fear and move on before life would start giving back.

After all the turmoil, the new owner and his general manager came into my office and explained what had happened. With heavy emotional humidity in the air, they acknowledged how difficult it may be for me, but they wanted me to continue to work there. In fact, they talked about expanding my responsibilities. Even though I was grateful for the way they viewed me, my focus was still on my big picture. Like the Hue's vision on the path of life, it wasn't clear where I was going. I just knew it was going to be great.

In what felt like the blink of an eye, I was at my last module for my degree. We had to go to a campground, so to speak, at a Bible summer camp where we would be giving our final presentations. It was early April, and our group arrived the night before the presentation day. We decided to go out for dinner and drinks, as we had become quite close over the last fifteen months. As we reminisced about great times and how fast the process had moved along, I was asked about my presentation. It was very personal, and I wasn't prepared to go into detail ahead of time. So I told them, "It's something close to my heart."

The next morning came soon enough as we gathered in a large log cabin's great room, which had a beautiful stone fireplace. We all pulled up chairs, couches, and whatever was available. Though I was nervous, I felt my growth had been tremendous, and I was confident about my presentation. I knew the reports were supposed to be serious, but I was about to take it to a whole new level.

Our assignment was to think of two things: one item or person that changed our past and one that had or would change our future. I knew weeks before what I was going to do; whether I had the courage to do it was the only question. As we took turns around the room, there were a lot of generic stories, and I was surprised that there didn't seem to be much depth. Our group had become close, and I'd anticipated more emotional stories. I picked up on a fear of judgment swirling through the air.

When Eve asked for the next volunteer, I raised my hand, because I was starting to have second thoughts about what I knew was going to be an emotional presentation. I had trusted this group of people for fifteen months, and I knew this was going to shake me up.

When Eve called my name, I reached into my backpack and grabbed a red mechanics rag. The jokes began to fly as they thought it was a pair of red underwear. I laughed awkwardly as I started to talk. The room would soon go from laughter to tears.

I pulled out a standard open-end wrench. As I fidgeted with the wrench, the tears began to flow. "This wrench represents the relationship I had with my past employer. I have always been just a tool for his use. Like most men, he was fond of this tool, but at the end, it was still just a disposable tool to complete his dreams." After I paused after grabbing a Kleenex from a classmate, I noticed the box began circulating around the room. Tears were flowing freely.

I looked down at the floor to remove all eye contact as I collected myself. "I'm sorry. I knew this was going to be tough." I reached into the rag again, this time grabbing the second item: the chain from the chainsaw that nearly killed me. "This chain set off a series of events that I can clearly see as God's hand guiding me to where I am supposed to be. This is the chain off my saw that changed my life forever." I wiped my nose and paused to try to contain myself. "This accident has led to a chain of events, no pun intended, that is simply unexplainable. The miracles that have taken place to get me to this spot where I stand in front of you were with no doubt divine intervention. My life is brighter than ever, and I can't wait to live it instead of it living me. I don't know what's next, but I know I will not accept a good-enough outlook for my future."

As I went to sit down, there was consistent sniffling around the room. The next guy said, "Great, how do you follow that?"

We took a moment to settle things down, and classmates came up to me and gave me a hug. I felt like I had just watched a flower on the path of life blossom right in front me. The Hue was present, and after letting go of my past right then and there, I knew I had left my baggage behind at that crossroads on the path of life. I knew that if I could recognize and take responsibility for my life and let go like I just had, my life was going to be great.

A month later came one of my proudest days. It was graduation day and nearing my third Celebration of Life day in 2001. We were going to celebrate in a big way.

As I walked across the stage, I heard my son yell, "Go, Dad!" Tracy and our three kids got to see me graduate with a bachelor's degree in business management after a tremendous amount of hard work. It was amazing that, from our humble beginnings, our life was erupting because of the results of an accident that had changed my perspective. My parents, in-laws, and immediate family all went out to dinner after the event. If the Hue had taught me anything, it was to be grateful and enjoy my victories.

In the next few months, I still worked for the new owner of the business. Away from work, I continued to exercise my hand every day to build strength, and I read several books, building my understanding of the Hue. I also began writing and painting as hobbies. I still had several emotional moments, but whenever I slowed down to observe life as it was in that particular moment, God rushed in, removing doubt, fear, and judgment.

The openness in my heart and controlled ego allowed me to see and experience things I couldn't explain. My openness to life created an open mind, and I started to have visions again. I had recollections of the visits in the Hue—just a feeling or an energy inside me. These visions were like intense daydreams and would eventually lead to an incredibly moving experience.

Late in 2001, our country had just experienced the worst act of terrorism it had ever seen. Markets were crashing, and everything seemed to be in chaos. My job, even though it felt fresh with the new ownership, didn't feel like home. My brother encouraged me to look outside the industry, so I did. I figured out how to use online job searches, and within a couple of weeks, I had been to several job fairs.

I found myself overthinking this new direction, so it was taxing. This was a new experience altogether. Tracy and I continued to pray for the right thing to come along. A month later, I received a call from a gentleman who said he was a manager for a direct-written insurance company. After a few questions, he asked if I would be interested in meeting him for an interview.

I looked across the couch at Tracy, shrugged, and said, "Absolutely. When and where?" A few days later, I met with Joe in a local hotel lobby. I took a personality test and answered several more questions. He told me that if they were interested in moving forward, they would contact me in a couple of days.

When returning home, Tracy wanted details. "Well? How did it go? What company?"

I shook my head, questioning my experience. "Direct-written insurance? I think it went well, but I'm not really sure. He said they have a rigorous hiring process, but they do need someone in the Jackson area. I don't really know about me becoming an insurance salesman though." I set the day aside and marked it up in the experience column.

A day later, Joe called and asked if I could meet him at another lobby in Lansing. That Saturday we met for more than six hours. After doing most of the talking, I was not only hoarse but also starving. Joe was so focused on finishing those sessions that he didn't have any concept about taking a break to use the restroom or get a drink of water. He had his agenda, and he definitely wanted to get through it.

After a long and intense conversation, I drove back to my parents' house in Okemos, where Tracy was waiting for me. On the way there, I prayed, "God, I'm not sure if this is just for experience or my future, but please lead me to a better place. Lord, please be with my family and me. Guide me to see life on a grander scale. Lead me through this fear that I may see life as great as it is meant to be, amen."

Tracy was shocked by how long the interview had been, and the same questions follow. "Did you get the job? What took so long?" I had been talking for so long that all I could think about was getting something to eat.

The following week, I met with Joe two more times, including an in-home interview with Tracy. After seven interviews, including with a regional manager and a final interview with director of field operations, I got the job. This was a brand-new path, and even though I had to take a pay cut with a family of five, I knew it was my direction. It felt right, and the potential seemed unlimited. I knew this opportunity had been put in front of me so I would walk through the door of fear that still existed in my life. If I couldn't trust the lessons of the Hue, especially regarding faith, I had gained nothing. My decision was well researched and thought out with Tracy's help.

After getting licensed, I was flown to Minnesota to meet with the other trainees as we began our new careers. I sat on the bus with about ten others, and I just listened. I heard them talking about our diverse backgrounds, and I began to question my decision. Upon arriving at the hotel, I passed on going to dinner with them, because I had lost faith and allowed fear to creep back into my head.

As they went off to dinner, I called Tracy. "Trace, I think I made a mistake. These people seem to know a whole lot more than I do about banking, financials, and other stuff that I don't understand."

She answered quickly to remove any doubt about the way she felt. "Give it the two weeks of training. If you still feel this way, find something else. I love you."

Relieved, I replied, "I love you too!"

The next morning, the fellow trainees greeted me, asking where I went and telling me they wanted to hang out with everyone. Nervous, I lied, "I didn't feel so well, so I went and laid down."

After the first day, I knew I was going to be okay. I had made a close connection with three others immediately. Our connection would lead to supporting each other through studying and practicing for the job. Prayer, faith, and action continued to add stability to my new life.

Away from work, I felt that my spiritual growth had taken off. Visions, like vivid daydreams, continued as if they were a reminder of the lessons of the Hue. I felt they were directing me and keeping the awareness in front of me. The visions were so intense at times that I couldn't help but go into a state of tranquility. The stress of a new job had its moments, but the opportunity was like no other. My eyes had been opened to a much larger world and a grander view of the path of life. In my off time, I wrote letters of endearment to my wife. These letters fed off my emotional moments from the accident three years earlier. I couldn't help thinking about where life had been just a short couple of years before. I couldn't shake the deep love for my family or life itself. I couldn't help think about life without Tracy's love and support. I wrote about it so that if another tragedy happened, no words would be missed. Here is one of the letters I call "Unspoken Words."

To my dearest wife,

Another Christmas is going by, another year under our belt. This is written to you so you never have to wonder about the unspoken word. The feelings of love and words of compassion sometimes gets lost in the craziness of every day. We have beat incredible or even miraculous odds. God has given us the opportunity to be successful in life, and we have grasped it with both hands. The miracles of every day, waking up, our health, our children, and life itself will never be overlooked again after the wakeup call in 1998.

No matter what's going on around us, we have each other, a love that lives in body and spirit. God gives everyone certain gifts. Your God-given gifts complete me. The person I am today is because of you. There is nothing God has blessed me with that can match the gift of Tracy Allyson Lee.

The qualities you possess are forever engrained in my soul. You are caring, nurturing, forgiving, compassionate, and loving. You are the best mother I could ever ask to develop and teach our children. Every day you wake up and work hard. Every day you wake up and create a safe haven for your family. You are the kindest and most loving person I have ever known.

What you do for me is create a safe place—a place I know that I can be myself. You bring out the love in my heart. You allow me to be compassionate and open my heart. The words that go unspoken are my failures. You have taught me to be open with you, our children, and myself. Never forget the love that God has placed in your heart. We all have a place in his plan. You have certainly found yours.

The unspoken words and the actions of love that are never put in motion are truly a tragedy when you look at the limited time we have on earth. I did not want you to go another day without you knowing how I love and cherish you. I am because you are. May God continue to bless us in our journey of life.

I love you with all my body and spirit,
Billy

I wrote similar letters to our kids so that in the craziness of life, the unspoken word would never be missed; they would know how I felt about them. These framed letters have hung in their bedrooms since that Christmas.

9

A Life's Balance

*A*fter taking time to learn the basics of my new job, I started to believe that even the highest marketing goals would be attainable through faith, goals, and hard work. My spiritual growth, support from Tracy, and my faith were illuminating the way. Life was good. I had taken a leap of faith with a serious pay cut to obtain this job, and soon I was making three times my old pay.

I knew from the Hue that this wasn't by mistake. I made my first president's council during my second year of eligibility, and success, even though difficult, seemed imminent. After my third year and continued success in the job, Tracy and I decided to buy a new home. This home was the nicest we had ever lived in together. Daily life slowly crept back into a routine where awareness eventually slipped away. Even though the accident was only five years in the past, my ego had found its way back. The lessons of the Hue also seemed to fade away as success widened.

And success wasn't free. It came with pressure to continue to succeed at a very high level. I had built something, and I didn't want to lose it. I had upgraded my truck, Tracy's car, and now our home. If my connection with material things was first, I was on top of the world. My loss of perspective was soon followed by my lack of awareness.

Tracy and I hadn't had a large marriage celebration, most likely because no one believed we would succeed. We had spent our eighteenth wedding anniversary at Disney, and that vacation left me with an ambitious plan. With everything at work going so well, I started to put a dream of mine into action. I wanted to wed my beautiful bride again, but this time I wanted to blow the doors off with an over-the-top celebration.

We had become huge fans of Disney, so that's where I started. I planned an entire wedding, including a guest list, without Tracy knowing anything. The date was set: our twentieth anniversary in 2006. We would be in Disney with the kids, and we would renew our vows.

I ran all of the emails through my work, and I set up a separate credit card to handle expenses as we got closer to the date. The venue, dinner, cake, and fireworks cruise were all set to go, and all I had to do was keep it a secret for one more year.

After a couple of close calls, I had only three months left to keep the secret. Tracy had no idea of what was coming, and it was time for the dress. We were in Hawaii for president's council that year. When we went shopping in Wailea, I said she needed to buy a new dress for our special evening on our twentieth anniversary. She found two, a black one and a white one, and both looked fantastic on her. After some negotiation, I convinced her that the white gown had a slight edge. With three months to go, and with this secret that I held from Tracy about to ooze out of me, the dress was bought. The guest list was complete—all family. We had eighteen people that would be wandering around Disney for two days before the event, trying to avoid Tracy. The final details had been put in place, including a beautiful pink-and-white rose bouquet.

As we traveled to Florida, I verified the final details with all my contacts for the quickly approaching day. We arrived at

Disney, and everything was a go. For two years, this plan had been in motion, and the day had come to implement it.

As we got dressed that afternoon, I sent the kids off to dinner. Unbeknownst to Tracy, they had been picked up by the limousine and taken to meet the rest of our family. Tracy knew that I had a special evening planned for our twentieth anniversary but had no idea of the scale. With the two of us dressed to kill, the limousine pulled up to the front lobby at Disney's Boardwalk with plenty of onlookers.

"Is that for us?" she asked as she wrapped her arm around mine.

Holding back a wave of emotion, I said, "That is for us." I couldn't keep my eyes from tearing up, but I was able to contain the flood—for that moment anyway.

Excitement filled the limousine, and she asked, "Where are we going?"

I knew the big reveal was only a ten-minute ride away. With a steadying pause to contain my emotions, I said, "You will know very soon. Just enjoy the ride."

When the limousine pulled up to our stop, Tracy was so overwhelmed by the moment that she didn't realize we were being dropped off at the Grand Floridian Wedding Chapel. The limo driver opened the door, and I guided her out by the hand. As we stepped out, the sun illuminated the view down the walkway bridge to the chapel, which sat on a small island. It was welcoming us with arches adorned with beautiful white flowers blooming with purity in color and fragrance. The chapel was surrounded by blue water glistening in the afternoon sun.

As we approached the bridge, Tracy didn't notice the sign out front, reading, "Lee vow renewal." Arm in arm, we began our stroll over the bridge. She was caught up in the splendor as her blond hair flowed in the light breeze. She was unclear of what was happening until we approached the crown of the bridge, and our nephew, who was on top of Grandpa's shoulders, came into view.

"Is that—what the—is that Gehrig? What's he doing here?" Tracy grabbed me tight around the arm as more of the family started to come into focus at the entry of the chapel. I could feel the excitement. "What? What is going on? Where did all of our family come from?"

As the excitement took over and tears began to flow, I cradled her hands and directed her attention away from the chapel to bring us face-to-face. At the crown of the bridge, I took a moment for just the two of us. I knelt on one knee, fighting tears all the while so I could speak clearly. "Tracy, when we were married twenty years ago, nobody really celebrated our day. I didn't even give you a proper proposal. So today is our day." As tears were flowing freely from the both of us, I asked with a trembling voice, "Will you marry me?"

Overwhelmed by the moment, she stood me up in a storm of tears, "Yes, for sure, yes." As she hugged me, I could see in her eyes that she loved me, even though she wasn't aware of everything that was happening.

As we finished walking across the bridge to the chapel, the rest of the family came into view from behind the flowering bushes, opening the floodgates. We greeted and hugged every family member that had made the journey to celebrate this day with us. We were in heaven on earth. Everything had come together.

Of course, Tracy didn't know this was just the beginning. As the family went inside and sat down in the chapel, the wedding coordinator and pastor filled us in on the ceremony. "I'm guessing you didn't know about this?" He hugged Tracy and gave me thumbs-up.

Tracy was still wiping away tears as she glanced up at me. "No idea! I can't believe our families are here!" Giving me a love punch, she added, "Where did you hide them?" The coordinator followed close behind with hugs and tissues, getting Tracy ready to walk down the aisle.

With Tracy's face still flush from the surprise, we walked up the aisle, hand in hand, passing by all our family members and our three beautiful kids, who were in the front row. As we approached the steps leading to the chancel where we would confirm our love, Cinderella's castle filled the chapel window. We faced each other as I held her trembling hands. I could see she was fighting to keep it together, but I knew my next surprise would end that fight. Tracy and I went through our vows, and I had asked the pastor to do a ring ceremony. After she slipped my ring back on my finger, I pulled a new customized ring out of my pocket, which I'd had one of my new clients make for me months before.

As I slipped the ring on her finger, her jaw dropped, and the pastor said, "I'm guessing you didn't know about that either?" With her eyes filled to the brim, she simply shook her head. The waterworks began to flow, and the pastor turned us to our family and introduced us forever more as husband and wife.

The evening was capped off by a video of our past twenty years, a surprise honeymoon, dinner, a fantastic chocolate-and-white mousse cake, and a two-hour fireworks cruise in front of the Magic Kingdom. Life was blessed; it felt like we were on top of the world.

When the trip was over, we returned to normal lives that felt a little more special. The following year, I had earned president's council again, and life seemed to be on cruise control. I still maintained a spiritual center, even though it didn't seem as deep as it had been just a few years earlier.

Then I suddenly started having a vision. It was as real as any that had come before it, but it was different in one way: it was the same dream, as if it was on replay. Whenever my mind was calm, it was there. It was so clear I could see my accident over and over again, and the perspective was always from above. It seemed like the more I ignored it, the stronger it became. It was intense, as if I were living it all over again.

I tried to explain it to Tracy, but I failed every time to put it into words. I knew it was calling me. I didn't know how or why it was doing it, and I certainly didn't understand what God was trying to bring to my attention. I felt life was going along so well that I was just having a flashback to my accident.

I had written a new customer account earlier that year. I marveled at this business owner, Charlie. He had an accident when he was a child, and all that was left of his right arm was a stub at the shoulder. He performed work duties, including lifting parts and tools that a man with two arms would struggle to lift. I had known him for only a few months when I had a moment that chilled me to the bone.

I stopped by his shop for a routine visit to see how everything was going and walked into his office unannounced. I saw him sitting in his office chair, working a plan spec on the computer. He turned, looked me in the eye, and said, "Did I ever tell you"—he stood and reached out with his left hand to shake my hand— "when I had my accident as a boy, there came a point where I sat above myself. I could see myself running from the barn to the house and back again." His emotions started to take hold. "I literally watched myself go back and forth, trying to get help, with my arm wrapped up so I didn't bleed to death."

I was stunned. I barely had words as my eyes welled up. This was the exact scene in my vision after my own accident. It was also the daydream vision that had been reoccurring over and over again for the last several weeks: I sat above myself, watching what was going on with the emergency crew.

As I wiped away overflowing eye, I said, "Charlie, why did you just tell me that story, right here, right now?"

"I'm not sure. I just felt like I needed to tell you."

With my emotions running over, I reached out with my left hand and shook his hand. "Thank you." I was so stunned and overcome that I lost focus and needed to process what had just happened.

As I turned to leave the building, almost in haste, I realized there had been no conversation, just him telling me that story. I drove home in awe of what I believed was the Hue reaching out to me. I didn't know for sure, but I felt that God was reassuring me that my experience during the accident was real; it actually did happen. I felt that I was lacking details, and there was more for me to understand. I just didn't know what to do with that experience. Every time I tried to process it, I ended up in tears. My lack of awareness and perspective led to confusion.

As wonderful as life had become, my self-awareness was about to get a reminder about life's balance. I couldn't help but think back to that experience in Charlie's office. Had I stepped off the path of life again? Was I actually standing on the rocky part of the path with no self-awareness?

Work was still going well, and it was time to announce the earners of the newly renamed chairman's council. I was shocked that I was not on the list. Nobody, including my manager, had been aware that a small sale had lapsed two weeks before the deadline, so I was short for the year. After battling back and forth with home office, it was apparent that they were sticking to their decision, and I did not earn chairman's council.

As if that wasn't enough, a large audit came back from one of my largest customers, and I was being charged back a substantial amount of money because of a mistake made by an auditor from a year earlier. It would take me several months to pay back that amount. And the downward slide wasn't over yet.

Tracy had planned a blowout fortieth birthday party, and I couldn't focus on anything but money. The party was coming in two weeks, and the last dagger had already hit. I just didn't know it. I had just lost a large sale to a friend due to some questionable details. The loss of the sale was less damaging than who it was with and how it happened. It was more devastating than the other two put together, because I had considered him a friend. We had helped each other and vented about life and work issues. I was seriously hurt that someone I trusted could do that to my family and me. It only fueled my pool of anger and self-pity.

"All of this in thirty days? What can possibly be next?" I clenched my fists, wallowing in self-pity. The darkness of the mist was now in full control.

After my fortieth birthday, the reality of all that had happened started to consume my daily thoughts. Those thoughts, fueled by anger, created hypothetical situations to give me a feeling of control. I had forgotten the lessons of the Hue. I sat among anger, hate, and fear, and I never even thought about my accountability, perspective, or self-awareness. My mind continuously questioned, "Why me?" I struggled to put the pieces together for the next month. I reflected on the negative situations as if the recent precious days, including our vow renewal and my birthday, had disappeared completely. I carried this burden deep inside and was ashamed that I had allowed this to happen to my family.

Tracy and I needed to get away and have some time to ourselves. We had spent our honeymoon and vacationed regularly in Boyne City, a small costal town on Lake Charlevoix in northern Michigan, This small community has beautiful sunsets over the lake that always bring us serenity.

Even with our dwindling bank account, Tracy knew we needed a weekend for just the two of us. As we traveled up to Boyne, the tension in the car was palpable. I had directed my pent-up feelings at an undeserving Tracy. With fear clearly in control, I became irrational as I tried to explain why all of this had happened to me. I neglected to reflect back on how blessed life was, and I missed signs that may have kept me from getting back to a false reality created by anger. The Hue, prayer, and everything good seemed to be gone. Because I had no accountability or self-awareness, the mist had complete control over my life, and it had darkened my perspective and outlook. It was similar to the Hue's visions when I was unaware the mist was even present, and I was blinded by my own darkness, unable to see the greatness of the Hue.

When we arrived at the condo we had rented for the weekend, not even the serene view of glistening Lake Charlevoix could free me from my dungeon of self-pity. Tracy knew that I was holding everything inside and that I needed to get it off my chest, which felt like an overfull balloon ready to explode.

"Billy, we're here to get away and relax. You can't blame yourself, me, or anybody else for this chain of events."

As we stood in the living room, luggage by our side, I fumbled with the keys with my unfocused eyes looking down at the floor. My internal struggle had become my nemesis, and my mind contained a relentless flow of negative and self-serving thoughts. I fought with blame, anger, and a desire for retribution. The pressure inside was as great as any force on earth.

When I looked up into her eyes, I saw concern and an open heart waiting for me to accept her unconditional love. I couldn't even find the energy to embrace her. I knew this had to come to an end right then and there. My bruised ego battled a soft spirit that needed to be embraced.

In those moments, I battled back and forth with fear of rejection and her undeniable loving comfort. I wanted to run away from it, but as if God had encased my feet in cement blocks, I was going to stand in that living room in my winter jacket with my luggage at my feet until I let go. I couldn't rationalize my thoughts to understand how we had been at such a peak in our lives eight months earlier and now it felt like the entire world had crumbled beneath me.

"I failed. I completely failed our family." My head drooped.

With a soft touch, she raised my chin to bring us eye to eye. "What do you mean, you've failed our family?"

I turned my eyes away. "I have let our entire family down. I failed in my job, and I have put our family under financial strain." The tears rolled down my face as if to cleanse the guilt from my mind. Tracy embraced me, and I could feel the rush of positive energy flood into me, similar to the energy swirling through the Hue. God used Tracy to touch my soul. I said, "I don't feel like my life is even worth living. How could I have let this happen?"

Closing any gap left between the two of us, Tracy again gently raised my chin. "Look at me! You have not let anybody down, especially your family. You work hard and give so much back to your family. These events may or may not have been avoidable. Don't ever say that your life is not worth living. We still have each other and three beautiful, intelligent children that love their father very much. We have jobs, and we certainly have been through much worse. We don't always need to understand why; we just need to have enough faith to move forward."

As if a chord had been struck, the negative energy that I had imprisoned inside me for weeks left in one fell swoop, leaving me exhausted. I could hardly stand. With the fight gone from my body, I collapsed in Tracy's arms. The weight that I had been carrying around was taken from me. All I had to do was give it up.

Once my head was clear, the lessons of the Hue rushed in, and my healing began. I needed to let go of the victimization of the previous moments. The Hue had taught me that life is always bigger than any given moment. The energy given to those moments, by me, had created a victim. I had allowed other people's sympathy to fuel my self-pity. I had to acknowledge the pain that I felt and be accountable for it. I searched for a different perspective and realized, like it or not, the company had to hold the line. As much as I tried to see a different perspective on the sale by a now lost friend, I struggled deep down with it. I had to let go of the animosity, or it would hold me back for as long as I held on to it—weeks, months, or even years. I just needed to let it go so it wouldn't hold me down like an anchor and pull the energy out of my future.

Any one of these events or a combination of them could have created an anchor that would have continued to pull me down to the darkest depths. When self-awareness allowed my mind to be free, I realized the anchor was never attached to me. I had held on to it as it took me deeper and deeper into the darkness. When free from the control of the mist, I chose to let it go and come back to the surface for a breath of fresh air. God, through Tracy, brought the lessons of the Hue back into my life. Going to our little slice of heaven in Boyne City released that anchor.

The following week, the vice president of marketing, Pat, and my director of field operations, Chris, made a special effort to call me. They reminded me of everything I had accomplished and that the chain of events that had transpired was undeniably unusual and painful. The mist was still like a fog in motion. Some days it lingered like a heavy drape that had more influence on my perspective than other days when my mind was clear, and I moved forward.

Although I struggled from day to day, the call from two trusted individuals convinced me that I was still in the right place. Things had not gone my way, but I had to take responsibility for my feelings, deal with them, and lean on God, my family, and my friends. It was time to move forward and get back in the groove.

I began by repairing my attitude and changing my perspective so I could see all that was good in the world again. Letting go of the mist that clouded my life took time and hard work, but most of all it took faith and self-awareness. I needed to be aware when it was shading my present moment and darkening my horizon.

God had placed people in my life to catch me in my fall; I just had to let them participate. I had to be vulnerable and to be free of the darkening mist to let it happen. My ego would have killed all future progress.

Reminders of the lessons from the Hue were ongoing and filled my daily life as if I were back in the Hue itself. Freeing my mind from life's uncontrollable events and balancing my thoughts, work, and family were the keys that I sought to unlock my future. I now understood that I had to use the Hue's lessons constantly to keep my life in balance. It wasn't a one-time deal.

Balance became my foundation for lessons learned. I could step back and see the balance—or lack of it—in everything. This including my diet, prayer, religion, marriage, and job. Again the Hue had shown me the way. This had to become a practice, a way of life, of being aware of my everyday balance. It started with the love of God, Tracy, prayer, faith, and the courage to take action.

10

Reflected Peripherals

*I*n the years since the accident, I've had too many moments of reflection to count. To avoid a recurrence of past failures, I have to develop daily routines to help ensure that a reflective awareness stays with me. I'm not sure that a search for complete enlightenment is even possible in today's competitive world, but I continue to keep my balance in search of an ego-free life.

Every single day, I've been bombarded by uncontrollable events that could easily be consumed by my ego, leading the way back into the darkness of the mist. Simple things can do this, like inconsiderate people, business decisions that adversely affect my job, politics, and certainly the media. Before the accident, I thought I handled issues fairly well. But as I looked back, I saw that I was caught up in the nonessentials that most people use to define their lives.

After our marriage during high school, Tracy and I worked very hard to make life work. We had a deep understanding and love for each other from the beginning. That love was the foundation that moved us through some very difficult situations.

The lesson of the Hue was that comfort provides a foundation for stagnation in faith, passion, and vision. How many times I felt comfortable with where I was and stopped dreaming. I allowed my faith to wallow in the depths of boredom. Tracy and I had typical marital issues that could have derailed our relationship if we had let our combined ego separate back into two separate entities. I had to become vulnerable and allow her to support me as much as I was her protector.

I learned that fear is a huge motivator and is often used as a tool to manipulate people. Fear creates doubt, and doubt is the bulldozer of all dreams. Balance takes practice and patience. Our life together always felt like a blessing, even in times when I tried to screw it up as I lost focus on our life together. I felt like life was good, and there wasn't anything we wouldn't do to work hard enough to make it better. I am because she is. In moments of clarity, I love because she loves me. I am a good father because she is a great mother. I am driven because she supports my biggest dreams. My biggest fear is that somehow I will let her down, and I don't balance out the equation of love between us.

Even with a visionary mind, I didn't realize how grand life could be or was supposed to be. I lived in my small bubble, and that was my world, filled with my own comforts and limited views. My life bubble had family, preconceived notions about religion, fear of failure, and a daily life with limited dreams. After the accident, I noticed that all people have their own life bubble. They congregate and stay close to others that have similar outlooks on life, even if that means limiting themselves. Most people won't stray from others that live in similar bubbles, even if they disagree with some of their behaviors.

The core of one's life bubble generally keeps people from seeing a bigger world. Their ego assists in holding that illusion by reassuring them that they have more understanding of the world than the next person as well as a better job, a better parenting style, a stronger faith, and definitely a bigger ego.

I used to believe my bubble was huge and encompassed many of life's offerings. I felt it had a clear view of the world—only to find out that it was a darkened perspective created by my ego. When the accident stripped all ego and unnecessary thoughts, God's view swept in and filled me with humility and vision. My peripherals in life were wide open, which showed me that life was and is a never-ending story. The only restrictions are limitations based on my own thoughts.

When I observed life, not envying someone else's, I could see my own demise. My ego told me how great I was doing to the point that I stopped dreaming. Indeed, in my own little bubble, Tracy and I had done well, but the safety and comfort inside our bubble had restricted our perspective and growth. The Hue taught me that life doesn't stop moving. I'm either growing or withering. This is essentially a spiritual version of the cost of living. Life doesn't get less expensive. I have to continue to grow just to keep up with my own life's position, or I will fall back into stagnation.

The more God showed me, the more I wanted others to experience what I had found. I had a new sixth sense, so to speak. I could feel through others' spoken words. All of the nonsense and lack of feeling was visible, including fear. I found in the Bible new lessons often missed by the ideology and ego of humans, and I wanted to help others see a bigger world. I could see in them the very things that had restricted me in my past. I could see helplessness on the inside while my ego supported fortress walls.

The lack of accountability that I had been unaware of in my own life was now visible throughout the world, as if God had given me x-ray vision. At times this gift felt more like a curse, and I found out very quickly that people don't want to look too far outside their own comfortable bubble. Very few individuals want help. They don't want to see a different perspective or take accountability. People, especially those who are ideologically locked, can't or won't look beyond the cramped but safe vision they hold dear to their heart.

When traveling for business a short time ago, I met an interesting man. He was very open and seemed to be looking for someone to listen to his story. He told me about his family and his career in the auto industry. He had battled several types of cancer and had come out on top. However, he said he felt that God picked on him, and he didn't understand why. He started talking about the very basic ideology of Christianity: the pearly gates and meeting God. He talked about the better place than his life on earth. I carefully interjected about my accident and living life right now. (He was several years older than me, and I didn't want to sound disrespectful.)

I adjusted my seat as if I knew I was going to need a comfortable position. "Sir, everything ideology teaches is about living for an afterlife." Again I adjusted my seat so I could look him in the eyes. "Why do you think challenges come to us? Is it because we need to struggle so we can die someday to live in a better place? Several enlightened individuals have walked this earth. These individuals all talked about letting go and living an ego-free life, which is not easy. The search for peace comes from the soul, yet people live through the empowerment of their ego or the depths of guilt. What if heaven is the ego-free life?" Seeing his discomfort, I said, "People spend all their time thinking it is better somewhere else, and they need to struggle now. Don't spend all your time thinking, *Why me?* Think about how great it is to have experienced life with your three kids, six grandchildren, and a wife that still loves you."

As I rolled on, he listened intently. "Life may simply be about balancing everything, and by everything I mean ideology, family, jobs, children, the challenges in our lives, and even our greatest moments. Everything has a balance. A large amount of anything is not good if it doesn't have a counterbalance."

With a look of shock, he said, "I know. That really makes sense." But he seemed to sink slowly back into his thoughts about God punishing him.

Before we stood up to board the plane, I asked, "Do you think it was God making poor life decisions that created hardships and now he is punishing you, or was it the years of internalizing stress or poor diet or maybe even the lack of exercise, living with a burden of guilt or fear? These are that same battles that I struggle with every day."

I could see that he was intrigued, but as we parted ways, I felt he was still stuck in the same place. I wish to this day that we could have finished that conversation so that maybe, just maybe, I could have painted a different perspective for him.

If God wanted us to be closed off, he wouldn't have put endless possibilities in our life. The devil inside is the mist in everyone's life, the lack of accountability, self-awareness, and perspective. But above all, it is about balance. People always think someone else has it better. It can be about physical things, health, religion, or wisdom. Instead of creating a driving force to learn and become better, it often creates envy or division. Envy creates wasted thoughts and energy, and division stops all transfer of wisdom.

Just for a moment, I wanted him to see from a different perspective. I wished that I could have shared the world that the Hue showed me—a moment to be grateful for everything he had achieved and for the beautiful life that surrounded him. I realized that people seldom want help regarding their ego. A person can fill a room with positive energy and temporarily change the energy in others in any given moment, but if he or she doesn't have the disciplines to come out of the darkness, the positive energy will simply leave.

Being intuitive has gotten me in trouble several times. This time it was with people that use social media to broaden their ego. As the ego constantly looks for reassurance and differentiation, social media provides both. I realize that there may be people out there that can balance their relationship with social media, but I haven't found one yet. It has enhanced people's self-image, no matter how far removed from reality it is. They have multitudes of friends—not real friends, just followers. These are people just like them that have a gaping hole in their life. So instead of addressing the gaping hole, they find cyber friends that fill the hole with acceptance, sympathy, and compassion. Everyone needs a hug at times or a little extra attention, but social media allows for the balance to be thrown off.

When too much sympathy leads to a lack of healing, the hole becomes self-pity. "Everyone out there feels sorry for me, so I must be right." Everyone knows people that are so intertwined in self-pity that they continue to spiral downward. New diseases are imagined, and more and more doctors appear to be uneducated about those special unknown conditions. The pool of self-pity that's enhanced by a limitless sea of cyber friends destroys awareness and perspective, not to mention accountability.

Lean on real-life family and friends to help you through tough times. Believe me, if you want to be right, someone will tell you how right you are, even if it's untrue. Accept your hugs in life when needed, but flip the switch by being accountability for your life through self-awareness. And no matter how difficult, find a new perspective. Remember, faith in God is just hope without action. God's gifts require action, and I was guided by a spiritual force to realize these gifts.

It didn't take long for me to recognize that God intervened through the accident to gain my full attention; it was possibly my last call in life. If I would have walked away, continuing to live the way that I was, who knows where I would be today. I could be overly optimistic, but it wouldn't be anywhere near the place that I am with my family, my understanding of God, my marriage, and life itself. The twenty-twenty hindsight chain of events was clear in my mind. The divine intervention had become intertwined as if I was being shown the way, even when I didn't recognize it. When I created a wall of protection around myself made of comfort and pain, I chose to be just okay with where I was in life. My new direction became clear and was undeniable.

That undeniable path started with me surviving the chain-saw accident. How I made it up the hill and was able to keep my head enough to know that I needed to kneel on my arm to keep from bleeding to death continues to marvel me today. Then the doctors repeatedly told me I would have no use of my left arm. If they could save my arm, I would have a useless hand. But a nerve miraculously regenerated, which was beyond the belief of some of the greatest surgeons in the world.

The next directive, believe it or not, was my long-time boss firing me. Nobody understood it, but it had to happen if I was going to redirect my life. After he fired me, I went out and created a business. This reminded me that I could be successful on my own. It also taught me that success isn't tied to happiness or my future path. That small part of my journey taught me, like a light bulb illuminated a new path for me, that I was courageous enough to do something else with my life.

Tied to that, a moment of guidance came when my previous boss called me out of the blue to talk about a job and gave me a message from a local college. I had made the call a year earlier, and the thought of finishing my education was nowhere on my radar. I got into a class with a professor that filled our class with hope. Beyond the standard education, I learned about centering my life and how to work on my self-awareness and how to let go of the pain from the past that was holding me hostage.

This led to a new career in an industry that I knew nothing about and that has taken me to heights I never dreamed of, expanding my horizons. The awakening with a client, as if I was getting off track again, reminded me of how big and powerful life is if I allowed myself to be connected to God's energy. It also brought my mind back to searching the depths of life. How far can I go?

One of the toughest months of my life, described in the chapter about balance, could have derailed my growth after the accident. I can't say that in that moment at the condo in Boyne City I contemplated suicide, but the door was definitely in front of me. I had allowed the darkness of my ego to control my thoughts and actions, and it was leading down a path of darkness. Having the love of Tracy and God in that room at that moment was the only thing that led me out of my ego's grip. I was so physically weighed down by the weight of my ego telling me I had let my family down that I nearly missed the greatness of life around me. It still threw me for a loop, but the accountability, awareness, and perspective brought me back to center, and faith followed by action created more personal achievements than I had thought possible.

My greatest years came after that devastating ego check. Did I want to sink or swim? My ego made me feel better but only added baggage that caused me to sink. When I released my baggage through prayer, love, and vulnerability, I could feel how light I had become as I soared to new heights. I came to a conclusion as I continued to fight for balance every day: when I notice, criticize, or judge the faults of others, I'm seeing the weaknesses of my own reflection.

Finally, the world has a way of balancing itself. Whether you, I, or the world take the time to see it, everything has a balance. Nature is constantly balancing itself through life and death. Every fall, the tree leaves in Michigan change to a beautiful array of colors and die off, only to return in the spring full of new and vibrant life. That balance restores itself through the weather, famine, and in some cases, disease. Make no mistake; the human desire to control everything has its balance point. Take the time to sit back, remove thought, and just observe. Soak it all in, and let it fill you up. I have been through a life reset, and I have lost my perspective from time to time. My key is to keep life's balance through accountability, self-awareness, perspective, and faith. The only way to do that is to release the ego. No matter how dark the mist appears, the Hue is constantly working. I just have to keep my tools in front of me, have faith in God, and take corrective action. One of the most difficult things to keep in front of me is the fact that the Hue is constantly working, even behind the darkest of mist. (Faith)

Always be grateful for your life and others in it. Never allow the mist of your ego to take that away. These tools, which take daily practice and prayer, will bring you back to God, faith, and family. If you're blessed with ego-free wisdom, use it to elevate others, not yourself.

CPSIA information can be obtained
at www.ICGtesting.com
Printed in the USA
FSOW01n1732120417
33046FS

9 781512 779783